KAREL ČAPEK

TRAVELS IN THE NORTH

EXEMPLIFIED BY THE
AUTHOR'S OWN DRAWINGS

Translated by
M. & R. WEATHERALL

London 1940
READERS' UNION LTD
by arrangement with
GEORGE ALLEN & UNWIN LTD

First published in Czechoslovakia under the title of "Cesta Na Sever"

MADE 1940 IN GREAT BRITAIN
PRINTED BY KIMBLE & BRADFORD LONDON W.1
FOR READERS' UNION
REGISTERED OFFICES: CHANDOS PLACE
BY CHARING CROSS LONDON ENGLAND
POSTAL AND ADMINISTRATIVE ADDRESS: DUNHAM'S LANE
LETCHWORTH HERTFORDSHIRE

CONTENTS

I

The Journey North

I

The Journey North

This journey began a long time ago in the days of my early youth; where are those times when we used to

sail out from Göteborg on the *Vega*, or from Vardö with the *Fram*! "In front of us was the quiet, open sea";

yes, those were beautiful days. But life is unaccountable, and adventurous; it is only a matter of chance that I have not become an Arctic explorer. And yet in those days, amidst the eternal ice, there was an unknown land waiting to be discovered, 89° 30′ North; it had a volcano on it which warmed my island to ripen the oranges, the fruit of mangoes, and of other plants still only partially known; and an unknown but highly civilized race of people dwelt there, living on sea-cows' milk. Perhaps no one will ever discover that island now.

My second journey North took longer, and most probably it will never come to an end; its harbours and stations are called Kierkegaard, and Jacobsen, Strindberg, Hamsun, and so on; I should have to cover the map of Scandinavia all over with names like Brandes and Gjellerup, Geijerstam, Lagerlöf, and Heidenstam, Garborg, Ibsen, Björnson, Lie, Kielland, Duun, Undset, and I don't know what besides; for instance, Per Hallström, and Ola Hansson, Johan Bojer, and others, like Andersen-Nexö, and the rest. As if it were only for a short time that I have lived on the Lofoten, or in Dalarne; as if it were only for a short time that I have run across Karl Johans Gate! It's no use, some day you have to go and have a look, at least at some of those places in the world where you are at home; and then you marvel, and waver in double amazement; that you have already seen it before, or that you couldn't imagine it at all. That is the strange thing about great literature: that it is the most national thing that a nation possesses, and at the same time it speaks with a tongue which is compre-

Sweden

hensible and intimately familiar to everyone. No diplomacy, and no League of Nations is so universal as literature; but people do not attach enough weight to it; and so they can always still hate one another, or be like foreigners to each other.

And then there is still another journey, or pilgrimage North; this makes for nothing else but just the North; because there are birch trees and forests there, because grass grows there, and plenty of blessed water is sparkling there; because there is a silvery coolness there, and dewy mist, and altogether a beauty that is more tender and more severe than any other; because we, too, are already north and carry deep in our souls a fragment of our cool and sweet North which does not melt even in the swelter of harvest; a bit of snow, a strip of birch bark, the white bloom of parnassia; the pilgrimage to the white North, the green North, the exuberant and melancholy North, to the terrible and lovely North. Not laurel, and olive tree, but alder, birch and willow, spikes of willow-herb, heather with its tiny flowers, hare-bell, and aconite, moss, and fern; spiraea by the streams, and whortleberries in the woods; no flaming South is so copious, and buxom, so juicy with sap and dew, so blessed with poverty and beauty, as the land of the midnight sun; and when you make a pilgrimage—but it is a sweat, man; a dreadful trouble and worry; and then when you make a pilgrimage, let it be right into the loveliest paradise; and then say if it isn't what you were looking for. Yes, thank God, it is it; I have seen my North, and it was good.

And there is still another journey North. People talk such a lot nowadays of nations and races; at least you ought to have a look at them. For my part, for instance, I went to have a glimpse of pure-blooded Germans; I have brought away the impression that

Norway

it is a splendid, and brave race, which loves freedom, and peace, makes a point of personal dignity, will not allow itself to be ordered about too much, and has not the slightest need of someone to lead it. When you set out on a pilgrimage in search of knowledge about different nations, do have a look at those that are happier and mentally adult. I went to have a look at the midnight part of Europe; and thank God, it's not so bad with her yet.

II

Denmark

II

Denmark

And you cross the Swedish frontier and [illegible] further on [illegible] there are even sandier [illegible] country [illegible] black and white cows [illegible] and here the red ones, and there the [illegible] look like [illegible] of land [illegible] Why not [illegible] black and white cows [illegible]

II

Denmark

And you cross the German frontier, and wander further over the Jutland soil. At first sight there isn't even such a striking contrast; on both sides of the frontier it is the same plain, undulating gently, just enough so as not to allow you to say that it is as flat as a table; the same black and white cows on either side, only over there the postmen have dark-blue coats, and here fine red ones; and there the stationmasters look like stationmasters, while here they remind you of kind and elderly sailor captains. Men alone with their governments and diverse regulations create big and sharp differences in the world. Why not purse our lips, and whistle cheerful tunes as these black and white cows mildly turn their Danish eyes towards us?

A small, light-green country, as plains are coloured on the map; green meadows, and green pastures, dotted with herds; the dark danewort with its white patches of bloom, blue-eyed girls with milky complexions like felt, slow and sensible people, a plain that you might draw with a ruler—somewhere near, they say, they have a hill, which they have even called Himmelbjerg; a man I know searched for it by car, and when he couldn't find it, he asked the people which way he ought to go; and they told him that he must have passed over it several times. But that doesn't matter; instead you can see well into the distance, and if you stood on tip-toes perhaps you might even see the sea. Well, why not, it is a tiny land, even if altogether it can count five hundred islands; it is a small slice of bread, but thickly spread with butter. And praise to the blessing of the herds, barns, and full udders, the church towers amidst the crowns of the trees, and the windmill sails reeling in the fresh breeze.

But by then we had already crossed the nice new bridge over the Little Belt, and we were on the island of Funen; which looks more like a garden than ordinary land. Well, yes, I ought to wander along that gentle road between the willows, along that road between the alders, along that road to the church tower on the horizon; but we are only here in transit, dear road, for our pilgrimage leads us to the midnight sun. And there are no villages here, as with us at home,

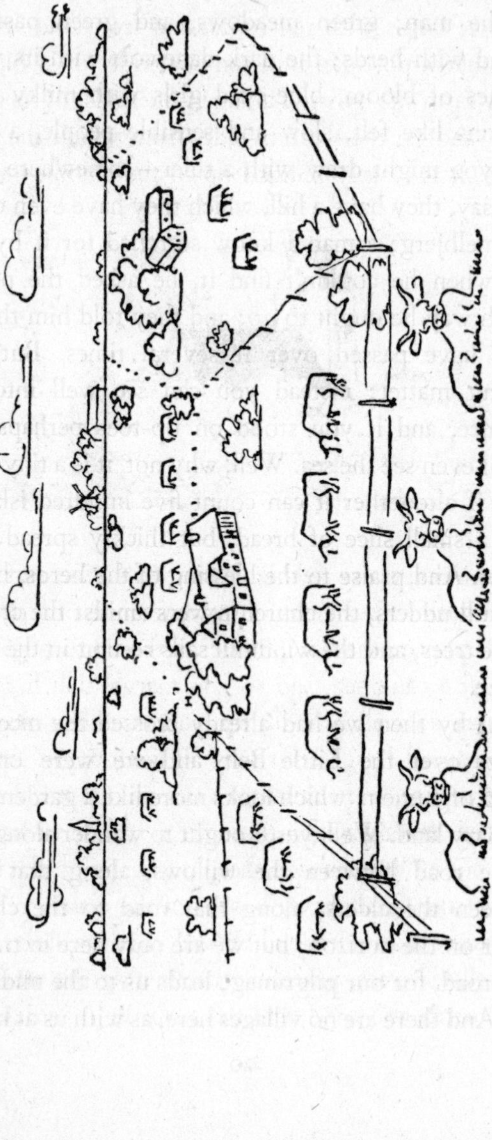

but only farms dotted one by one over the green pasture; farms with red roofs; and from one farm to the other a postman in a red coat rides on a bicycle. Every farm sits by itself alone in the midst of its green fields, and on the western side, from which the wind blows, it is closely muffled up to the chimney with a

belt of trees; every field is fenced with wire, and slow horses with white manes, or red cows in an orderly row graze upon it; they are, in fact, tethered to pegs, but those you can't see, and so you marvel that here the cows are so well brought up, and that they graze in regular, model ranks. Or they all lie down in equally serene repose, and ruminate in unison. Or it is a flock of sheep, among which there are no black or mangy ones, but all little chosen sheep pasturing on the right hand of the Creator. Or bushes of the common elder graze there motionless and blissful, round willows, and fat, well-fed trees, peacefully ruminating the moisture of the earth, the wind, and the silver light of day. All

God's pasture. Nothing but a large holding of God on which not even the work of man is visible; so skilfully and tidily it is done.

And in fact it looks as if it had been taken from a huge box of toys, and spread out neatly over the gentle plain; here you are, children, you can play; there are houses and stables, brown cows, and horses with white

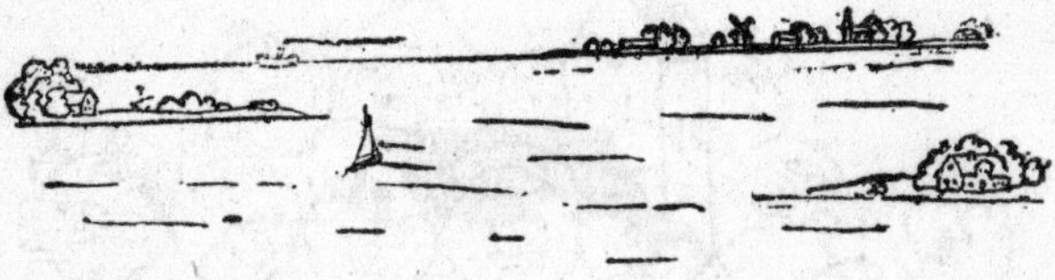

manes. Here you have a white church, and I will tell you why it has got thirteen notches in its tower: they are the twelve apostles, and at the top is Jesus Christ himself. And now set them out over the green pasture in rows and squares so that it looks nice and full; put a windmill here, and there a postman in his red coat, there bunchy trees, and put some figures of children here who wave greetings to you (yes, there must be a train here); and now tell me if it isn't a beautiful game! Well, yes, isn't it Odense, Andersen's town; that's why the toys have come to life, that's why the cows flick their tails, the horses raise their beautiful heads, and the figures of people move from place to place, even if gently and without noise. This then is Funen.

And because it is Funen we must put round it the

sea; the smooth and clear sea, and on it the toy boats, the white plumes of sails, and the black veils of steamers; and because it is a game we will push our train on to a boat and go by train across the sea. Didn't I say that it was a game? For the boat is full of children, the boat puffs across the Great Belt with a load of kiddies, blue-eyed, freckled, fidgeting and chirping

youngsters, little girls, red-haired ones and pickles, they swarm like chickens into a coop. God knows where they are taking this kind of merchandise; all the sea-gulls from over the Belt have hastened here to have a peep at that human fry, and they accompany the boat like a gigantic flag, fluttering and clamouring.

Those straight, very low lines on the horizon, that's Denmark; there's Funen behind us, and Zeeland in front, and Sprogø, and Agersø; you wouldn't believe that men, cows, and horses could live on that flat line. So look at it, all Denmark is made out of the horizon net and without discount; but instead, how much of that sky they have above their heads!

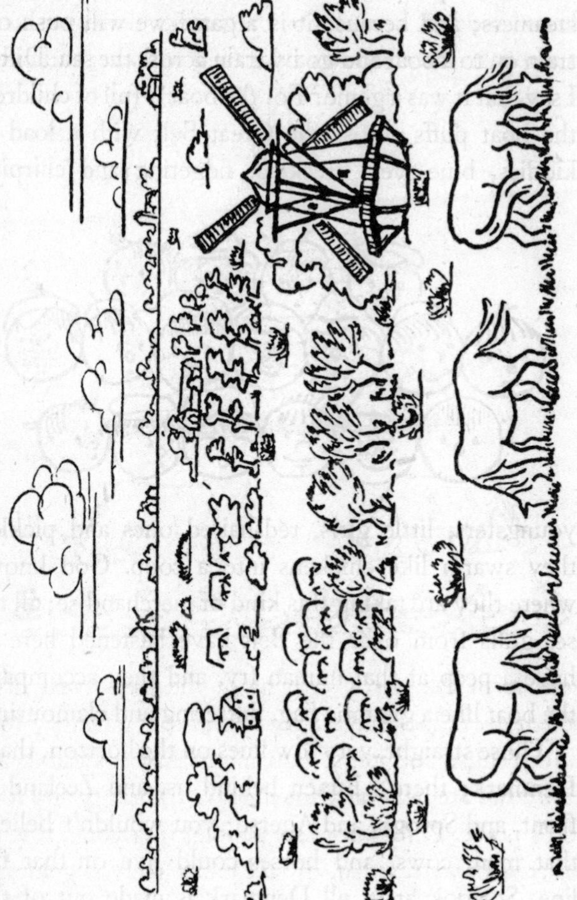

Zeeland, a green pasture of cows, sheep, and horses; look what a smiling land, all cows, all cows, what a blessed land of cows! On the baulks danewort and hautboy, in the meadows alders and willows; and over

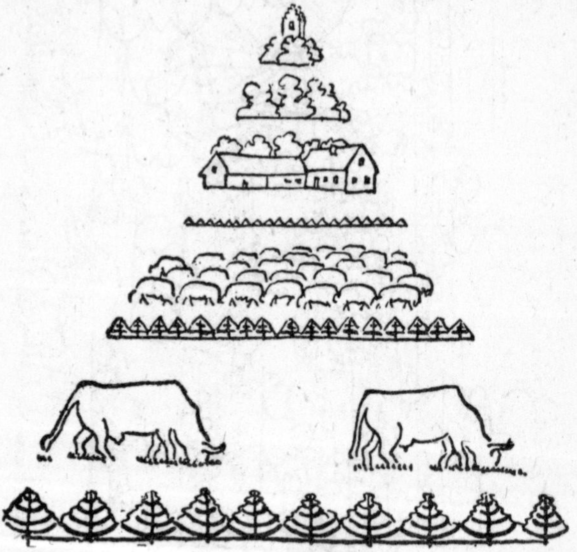

every farm the bushy crowns of the trees, vast like cathedrals. It looks like a park, and it is a factory for butter, eggs, and pigs; you might say instead that these cows are here only for the sake of beauty and for God's peace. Only very few people; if anyone, it is a gardener in a straw hat, or still more likely, a gelding with a white mane that gazes seriously and wisely after the receding train and shrugs his shoulders. Why such haste!—Well, to have a look at the North,

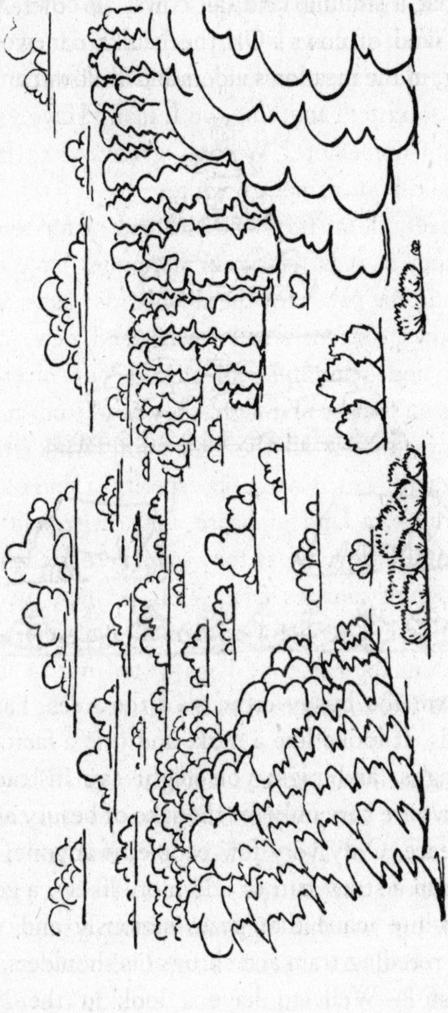

gelding!—And what there?—To look and learn how people, horses, and reindeer live up there. Reindeer? What's that?—They are a kind of animal, gelding; they have antlers, and pull sledges, as you do.—I don't pull anything, do I, man? Have you seen a draught-horse here? We only graze and at times we meditate till our manes go white.

A sweet, clean, tidy land; instead of fences young little pines as it is when our mummies have cut out notches in the paper for the sideboards; cows and still more cows, ancient small towns, and new farms, a church, and windmill—all spread out nicely at a distance so that at first sight they might be small like toys from a box; all the time more Andersen than Kierkegaard. Yes, a land of prosperity, a land of butter, and of milk, a land of peace, and of geniality. Yes, but then tell me why, as they say, there is the highest percentage of suicides here? Well, perhaps the reason is that this is a land for contented and quiet people, eh? An unhappy man perhaps would not fit in here; he would feel so ashamed of his distress that he would die of it.

And something more: Danish woods. They aren't really woods, but groves; beech groves and oak minsters, crowds of alders, fleecy coverts, and Druidic sanctuaries of ancient trees; lovers' groves, groves of worship, but not that big, murmuring element that is called a wood. As a whole a tame, pleasant and kind, mild and decent country; you wouldn't even say a country but a good big farm which the Creator Himself has taken pains to cultivate, and so that man might farm it well.

KØBENHAVN

A fat peasant child with a head too big, and too intelligent: that is Denmark. Imagine, a capital with a million inhabitants on a body of a nation of three millions; a handsome town, royal, and almost new, lively and spacious. Only a few hundred years ago, they say, Copenhagen used to be locked up for the night, and the Danish Mr. King used to have the keys of the town gates on his night table. To-day, no longer are there any town gates, and Copenhagen is called the Paris of the North. (In the Lofoten, and in Vesterålen they call Tromsø the Paris of the North, but there conditions are rather different.) Copenhagen to-day is reputed to be a flighty town, nay, even profligate; and so a bad end is prophesied for it too. In fact they have there an equestrian statue of a king; and because the statue is made of lead, that leaden horse has worn himself sore under that leaden Mr. King, and his belly is slowly and constantly nearing the ground. When, they say, his belly touches the pedestal the downfall of Copenhagen will take place. And, in fact, under that statue I saw old and younger people sitting long into the night; perhaps they were waiting for that sign of destruction.

When one speaks of Copenhagen, one thinks of

Copenhagen porcelain; but there are many other things worth noticing, especially:

1. Men and women on bicycles. There are as many here as in Holland, and they rustle through the streets in whole swarms, in streams, or more or less combined

in pairs. Here the bicycle has ceased to be a means of transport, and has become something like a universal element along with earth, water, fire, and air.

2. Fashion Shops. I have never seen anywhere so many shops with women's fashions as in Copenhagen; they are just a collective phenomenon like the public houses in Prague, or the coffee-houses in the harbours beyond the Arctic Circle.

3. No policeman in the streets. "We can look after ourselves."

4. The Royal Guard in huge bearskins. I have seen

twelve of them, they were an imposing sight. "Here," said our guide, pointing proudly, "you see half of our army."

5. Art collections. Anyone who wants to see French sculptors, Falguière, Carpeaux and Rodin, or who

is interested in Paul Gauguin, must go to Copenhagen. That all comes from beer. Here it is the big Carlsberg Brewery from which most of the profit goes to the famous Carlsberg Fund for the encouragement of art and science. God, if we at home drank for the benefit of art, there would be some statues and paintings! But Carl Jacobsen and Mrs. Ottilie aren't found in every country! That would be too grand.

6. Svend Borberg. He is a newspaper man, writer, dancer, actor, and sculptor, grandson-in-law of Ibsen

and Björnson, a lean and splendid man with the face of a diplomat from the time of the Congress of Vienna. Those of you who have seen Copenhagen, and have not met Borberg, don't know anything, and you have been running round Tivoli from Vesterbogade right

to Amalienborg to no purpose; but in spite of that, you can go to Tivoli, for

7. Tivoli is the capital of Copenhagen, a town of swings, shooting-galleries, fountains, bars, and entertainments, a town of children, lovers, and altogether of people, a great amusement park, perhaps unique in the world in its popularity, popular heartiness, and its naïve, gay, kermess exuberance—

8. And what else? Yes, canals, and fish markets, royal palaces, and sailors' pubs where the concertinas drone away into the transparent night; venerable

old houses of merchant gentlemen, runic stones, and cheerful girls in printed frocks from the fashion shops, fat and healthy children—

9. Yes, fat and healthy children, fed on cheese and milk like the Copenhagen Anneke from a bright little Danish house drawn here on approval.

10. And no beggars, altogether no speck of grime and misery; the other day they only found sixteen people who had no roof over their heads at Christmas. And no one looks at you with distrust; you ask for whisky in the bar, and they bring you a whole bottle; but you'll tell us afterwards how many glasses you've had. Let me tell you, it would be a good life for a man; but it's no use, my friends, we are only here a moment, and in passing, well, then, fare you well.

11. Just one last stroll along Langelinie, to see through the transparent northern darkness how the glistening steamers sail to Göteborg or to Malmö; it is strange, we always envy the boat that is sailing out and the shore that is slipping away.

* * * * *

And still Helsingør, Hamlet's Elsinore, and Kronborg castle. Still the Danish beaches on the mother-of-pearl sea, thatched Danish cottages in a blaze of rambler roses, beech groves, and herds of brown cows. And then Kronborg, or Elsinore rather. Admittedly it doesn't look like a melancholy prince here, except in being so terribly big; and on the bastion where the ghost used to haunt there are eight guns now, and one little Danish soldier peers threateningly at the opposite Swedish shore. In the old days they used to levy a ship-toll here; but now they only fire a salute when a man-o'-war is sailing by. There won't be any more fighting here.

So that now is the Swedish shore, that low blue line opposite; and after the Danish manner we bid a nice farewell to the dear and kind land which we shall leave behind us. Then we raise a glass of aquavit, and become terribly serious, with lips held tightly, and our eyes fixed as if a deep thought were being born; then we look steadfastly, ardently, and a little as if in amorous exaltation, into the eyes of Sven Borberg, we whisper "*Skaal,*" and the aquavit is poured into our throats with a graceful bow. It is a bit difficult, especially if you do it often and to the bottom. And for a long time yet the conscientious pilgrim will remember the only Danish mountains which he climbed with groans and difficulty. They were the mountains of food.

III

On the Other Side of the Öresund

III

On the Other Side of the Öresund

It is only a jump from Denmark to Sweden, especially if you make the jump in question from Copenhagen to Malmö, or from Helsingör on to Helsingborg; all the same, having made contact with the Swedish soil, you must fill up a voluminous questionnaire, who you are, and where have you been born, and why have you been born, and after all what do you want in Sweden; perhaps the reason is because officially they make a note if perchance you aren't a Danish King coming to conquer the plains of Sweden, as they used to do in history.

For here once upon a time the Danes ruled on both sides of the Öresund, and they collected the toll, mentioned above, from the trading ships; that is why on this and the other side of the Sund the contrast in scenery is not so striking. A pleasant, gentle plain, only undulating slightly so that you aren't able to say that it's as flat as a pancake; on the fields herds of piebald cows, in the crowns of the trees the serrated

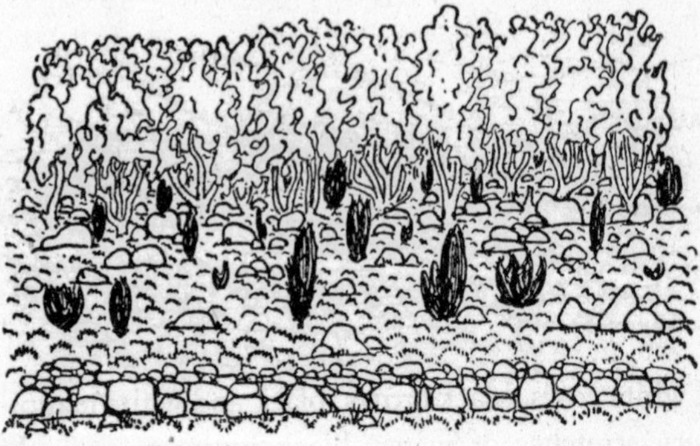

towers of churches, windmills with sails, and white cottages and farms dotted here and there, huddled among oak trees centuries old; and plenty of the bounties of God, if it is a case of full udders, wheat, and rich meadows. But suddenly instead of white cottages you see wooden buildings painted red, and nicely framed in white round the windows and gables; a silver birch flashes by, always more and more birches, always more dark woods, birches with silvery bark, and red painted buildings; the earth gathers into mounds, and hillocks, and here and there boulders of granite emerge. And always more of that granite.

The Danes, I believe, never ruled here; if so there would not have been so many boulders; there are no boulders in Denmark, except on the barrows of the ancient heroes. Well then, this is Sweden, the land of granite.

Dark boulders and green pastures, dark woods, and silver birches, red cottages with white edges, black

and white cows, black crows, black and white magpies, silvery stretches of water, black junipers, and white spiraeas; black and white, red and green. And always more of those boulders; here scattered in the sea, here they pass into the wood, over there they sprout up from the earth in the centre of a meadow, or a field of rye; erratic boulders as big as a house, rubble and ground granite sheets; all stones, but no grown rocks; only rolled on, piled up, heaps of boulders, my friend, but it's all Moraine as it stands in the book; an ice sheet formed this land; only over there, on the Danish side, has it left a bit of space for the alluvium to show what it can do. But that is merely Cambrian and Silurian; While this, old chap, this is the oldest rock; where would chalk be here, or sandstone! Do you remember how at home, in the woods of your childhood, you

used to find erratic boulders of granite? There too, they say, they were brought by an ice sheet. So then we ought to be as if at home here in the Primary rocks.

As far as I have ascertained those granite boulders in Sweden serve partly, on the one hand, for erecting barrows and grave-stones of the New Stone Age, partly, on the other, for cutting runes, and finally for

making stone walls and fences round the farms and tiny fields. On such a field in the middle of the wood perhaps only a couple of boulders are growing, with juniper, and cushions of wiry grass, or moss, but it has a wall of stones as if giants (from the Old Stone Age) had collected them and piled them up; but as for the houses, they aren't made of cold stone here but of warm scented wood.

I never had enough of you, red and white edged Swedish homesteads and farms, so immensely uniform over the whole vast and spacious land of Sweden, and at the same time so infinitely and amusingly diverse!

The smallest wood-cutter's hut in the forest is made of planks, and painted red and white, just the same as

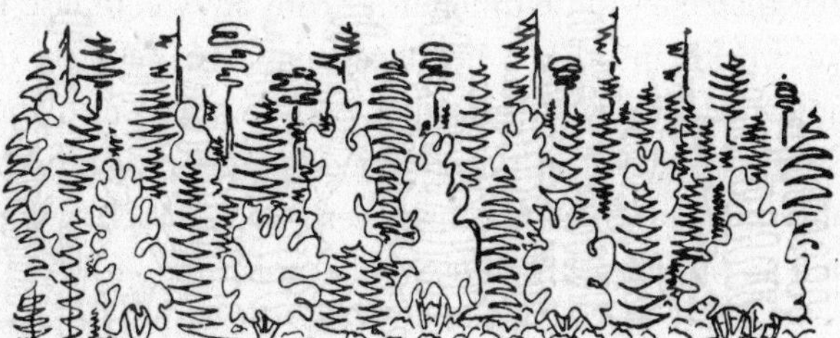

the most broad-shouldered and richest latifundium; but as there are not two human faces alike in the world, I did not see two Swedish farms alike in the thousands that I greeted along the road. Each is a differently composed cluster of dwelling-houses, stables, cow-sheds, barns, hay-lofts, and silos, drying-lofts, and outhouses, sheds, and hen-roosts; each has a different configuration of roofs, penthouses, gables, porches, and bay-windows. Here phantasy is almost inexhaustible, what to do with the windows, how to group them or to spread them out over the façade, and how to frame them: into the width or the height, into square, triangle, rhomb or semicircle, in twos or threes. I should have gone on for ever drawing it, but without the red, white, and green colour it's not the right thing; and besides, these houses pushed together, built up, and added to are a great nuisance with perspective. Therefore I have to let you stand, Swedish farms, amidst your pastures, granite walls, willows and ancient trees, and turn to something else, say, the woods or the lakes; only I still want to mention that the farmers here dry their hay quite differently from anywhere else in the world, and that is in shapes like a goat's back, on poles held together by wire, or laths; and also that Swedish sheaves of rye are dried on poles, most probably the reason is because there's too much wood, and an overmeasure of heavenly moisture.

And so that's why I shall say the important and greatest word: woods. They say that six-tenths of Sweden are covered with forests, but I think that there are still more of those woods; and these are the kind of woods which most probably grew in the first fifty or hundred years when Nature was only finding out how

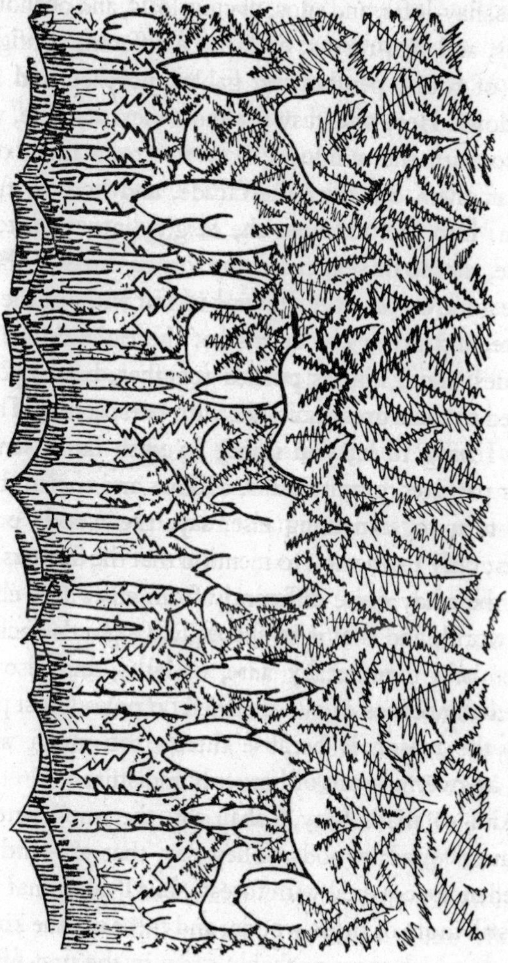

the northern growth is made; such an, should I say, abundance is here, of exuberant and original ideas. Not that there might grow, God knows what; without exception it is spruce and fir, pine, birch, and dark alder, not to speak of juniper; always, and endlessly, the same, but you don't grow weary of it, my friend, and you can't see the end of that abundance of vegetation. Moss up to the ankles, whortleberries up to the knees, and ferns very nearly up to your waist; the dark flames of juniper, whole coral of birches, dead wood, and uprooted trees, as in the virgin forest, heavy brushwood hanging right down to the ground; infinite and impenetrable forests growing for ever, old, and eternally being born, flourishing in their own way, so dense and compact that it is one mass. No young forest, young coppice, standards, and old trees as with us, but all the same time, and together; all together birches, and pines, and firs; all together forest, and wood culture, a Nordic jungle, a fairy-tale wood, a wood of gnomes and giants, a real Germanic wood, and a huge wood factory; elks, all chin and nose, with splayed antlers, are still running about here, and I shouldn't wonder very much if a wolf wouldn't also be here, Red Riding Hood, the unicorn, and other wild beasts.

Black granite, white birches, red farms, and dark wood: well, the silent lakes are still missing for the impression to be complete. At any moment it sparkles between the woods in the most varied dimensions and

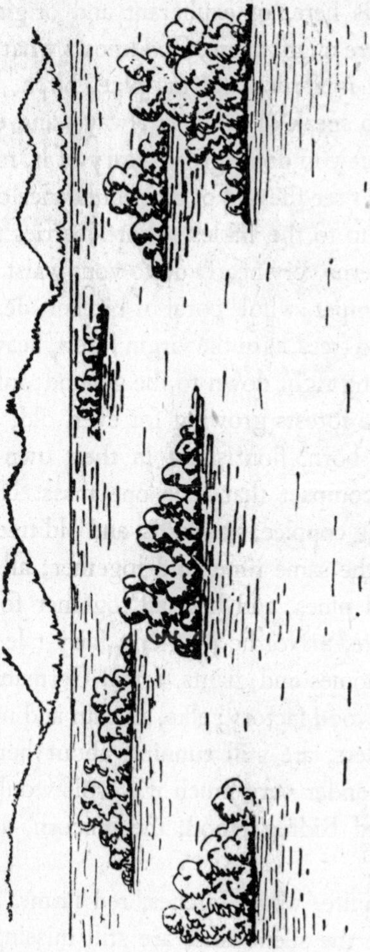

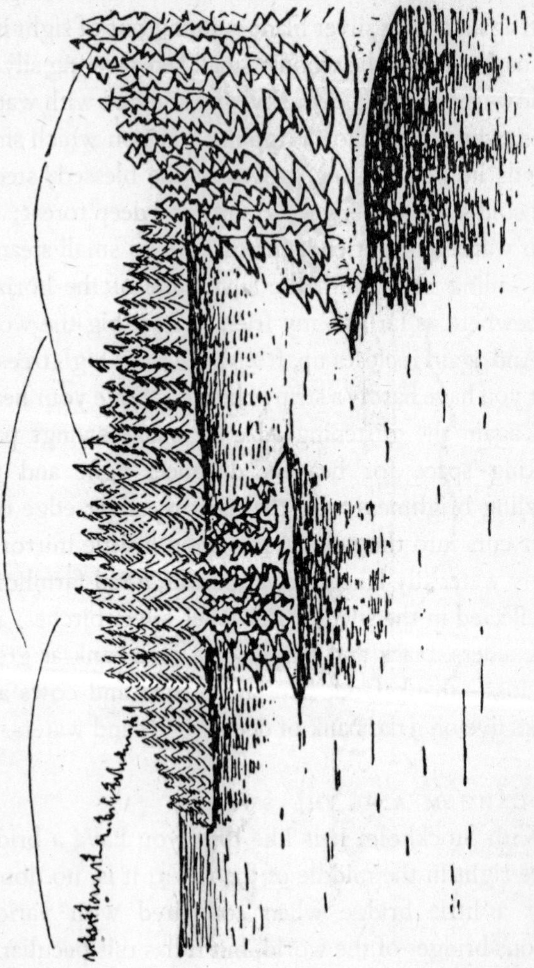

shapes: at one time a little black pool bedded in peat; then again a long silver blade running out of sight into the dark mass of the woods; small lakes among silvery willows mirroring a clear sky, and studded with water-lilies, white and yellow; rippling lakes on which small islands lie like floating groves of the blessed; steely, and cold surfaces between granite and deep forest; and then water without end, furrowed by a small steamer and sailing boats with the silver line of the horizon somewhere as far as—my friends, how big the world is! And again it closes up, from both sides high trees so that you have hardly a strip of heaven above your head; and again the glistening adze of a lake swings past, making space for heaven, distance, light and the dazzling brightness; and the narrow, silver edge of a river cuts into the woods, the smooth little mirror of a tiny water-lily lake gives a sparkle; a red farmhouse is reflected in the silent water-level, silver birches, and dark alders, black and white cows on a bank as green as moss—thank God, here again man and cows and rooks live on a flat bank of deep woods and waters.

STOCKHOLM AND THE SWEDES

With Stockholm it is like this: you have a bridge there right in the middle of the town; it is, no doubt, only a little bridge when compared with various famous bridges of the world, but it has this peculiarity that just along one of its sides the water floods away, and forms nothing but *viken*, and *fjärden*, and *sundet*, nothing but *sjön*, and *holmen*, nothing but bays and harbours, and channels, and islands till it gets to the Baltic Sea; and just on the other side of the bridge, that water again floods out for hundreds and hundreds of miles, and makes swarms of channels, bays, *sunds*, and *ströms*, nothing but *fjärden*, and *sjön*, and *viken*, and

holmen, which all together are called the sweet lake Mälaren; and because Stockholm is partly built on those islands, a foreigner is never sure whether at the moment he is standing on the mainland, on an island, or on a mere protuberance, in the sea, or in the middle of a fresh-water lake. With regard to those islands, and eyots, further away in the sea they are called *skären*, and there are so many of them that every well-to-do Swede can afford his own islet, and his own motor-boat, and can bathe from his own shore; there are as many of those motor-boats as there are flies, and any moment one of them is loudly and zealously chuffing away towards the rocky little island with thirty pine trees and a dwelling-house; but a postman must have a bad time here if he has to sail all over it every day.

Stockholm itself is a busy, tidy, and apparently a fairly rich town; it has crowds of bronze kings, cyclists, and handsome, leggy girls and fellows almost to a man larger than life-size; it is a perfect race, but they have no racial theory to account for it. Mostly tall, and fair-haired people with broad shoulders, and narrow hips; and usually silent. Here cars do not hoot, and chauffeurs do not swear; let everybody look after himself, and the others, greet them, and don't make a noise. Then there is the royal castle like a huge square letter-weight over the sea; Bellman's cellar where even to-day you eat well and drink well in memory of that Epicurian poet; in the Djurgården there are old oaks growing in memory of the same Bellman; on Skansen old cottages, and windmills brought there from all parts of Sweden along with old women in national costumes, polar bears, seals, elks, and reindeer; and in the Nordiska Museet a surfeit of folklore painted and carved—for that there must be those long northern nights so that a man might take his jack-knife and whittle, carve and shave, perhaps a treddle for the spinning-wheel, till it is etched out as fine as lace. And on the walls of the peasant dwellings long friezes of painted figures, so that in the northern night you would also meet processions of people. What creativeness in human nature! What naïve pleasure of things painted, and carved, hammered, embroidered and woven! From the Fiji Islands right up to the Arctic Circle it is really the same: man is here not only to make a living but to image the world and create things for their beauty, and for his own pleasure; but in these days he doesn't carve ornaments and figures, but mends his motor-bike, or he gains knowledge from the newspapers. What do you want, it's progress.

And then there is Östberg's huge Stadshus, the largest modern palace I have ever seen, with halls so majestic that they might be better for divine service, a World Congress, or even for some board of directors; gay streets with orange, blue, red shutters for all the windows; and the working-class quarters with serial houses built concertina fashion so that one person might not see right into his neighbour's windows; and the district for villas in the woods where from every house flies a cheerful little flag, and in every garden there is a tiny house just for children so that they can play in a world of their own; and a telephone which, when you want, tells you what time it is, and what sort of weather, which wakes you when you like and gives you messages when you come home; many new bridges, and new roads, little interest in politics, dogs without muzzles, girls without paint, streets without policemen, bathing huts without keys, gates without bolts, cars and bicycles in the streets with no one on guard, a world without eternal fear and distrust; and particularly the strangest thing, the immense northern day, and bright night when you don't care for going to bed, when you don't even know whether it's already to-day, or yesterday, and whether people are already on the move, or still on the move; it doesn't even get dark, it only turns pale, transparent, and phantasmagoric; it isn't darkness at all, but an odd, ghastly light without any source, which seems to rise up from the walls, roads and water

—then only the voices grow low and you stay sitting.

*   *   *   *   *

You stay sitting because in Sweden such hospitality prevails. For you are not to go to bed until after all the other drinks your hostess has offered her guests a cup of tea. With reference to the local customs, the guest sitting on the right side of the mistress of the house has to propose a toast or deliver a speech in which he does honour to his host, while the master of the house does the same to as many guests as possible, each in his turn; and as soon as the guests have put down their napkins after the meal they goosestep up to the mistress of the house to tender her thanks. This custom is said to have been handed down since the time of famine, I don't know in which century; but it must have been a long time ago, because to-day in times of famine people don't entertain any more, they sell. Altogether it seems in Sweden as if the people made a point of ceremony; they really are terribly dignified, and somehow stately by nature. In the local Tivoli I saw a Cuban jazz-band from Habana perform under the open sky; the people of Stockholm watched that band of Creol buffoons seriously and silently as if it were a sermon on Sunday. I am not quite the smallest of men; but among those long and silent

Swedes I felt like a babe lost in a wood. Or there was a squash for an open-air restaurant; and instead of arguing for a place, as they would have done in Europe, they stood in a queue, and waited patiently until some venerable dignitary took them to an empty table. If it is like this in everything it might not be difficult to be king here; for it is certainly not the worst job to govern people who are gentlemen.

God knows, I can't say that I gained an intimate knowledge of the Swedish nation, and of its ways and customs; but when one is a stranger and a wanderer, one observes small things, as for instance an inn or road; it is not the point that the inn is clean and good; that goes without saying; but you arrive and order *frukost* for two crowns and an odd ore, and now take from the big table in the middle of the dining-room what your heart desires; there is fish, salads, roast meat, cheese, bread, and ham, lobsters and crabs, herrings, and butter, and eels, so that you don't know what to take first; and then they bring you something warm in a dish, and when you have eaten that they bring a dish full of it again, and they are terribly pleased because you like it; and when you think that by now you have brought them to bankruptcy they bring you the visitors' book to inscribe in grateful memory. What the devil does it matter if you have eaten more than your fill; for here is something which isn't a matter of eating, but something that is priceless: respect and trust in the man, however strange, who comes into the house.

Or the road then: because they are making so many roads here you have to drive along all the time in narrow field tracks; and you meet a wagon which goes into the ditch to make way for you; you meet a car which at a distance backs so that you can drive through; and the other driver doesn't curse you at all, but he touches his cap, and greets you. And every man at the wheel greets another at the wheel who passes him; and he greets every cyclist and pedestrian. And these greet every carriage which stirs up the dust for them on the road. Petty things, I know; but the wanderer gathers a little flower along the road, and picks up some trifle to keep for a souvenir. And perhaps it isn't only a trifle if the wanderer in a very strange land feels more a man and a gentleman than anywhere else in the world.

ROUND STOCKHOLM

The surroundings of Stockholm, that is mainly the sea, and Mälaren, and various other lakes, and islets;

but at first sight you can't make out what is what; there is always nothing but little islands, spurs and bays, and round about woods and forests. Of course Mälaren is the biggest thing, and is to be found, as far as I can tell, on all sides, and altogether everywhere; never mind which way you travel out from Stockholm, you see the bay of a lake, and they will tell you that it is part of Mälaren. If I were a Swede, I should also regard the Baltic, Hardangerfjord, the Zuiderzee, the English Channel, the Atlantic Ocean with all its off-shoots, the Lake of Geneva, the Straits of Magellan, the

Red Sea, the Bay of Mexico, the Java Seas, and other waters as simply spurs and arms of Lake Mälaren;

such a large and wonderful water it is. So that you can also see how handsome it is, I have drawn on one sheet its various banks and eyots, together with suitable vegetation like spruces and pines, willows, alders, oaks, sedges and reeds, water-lilies and boulders.

In some places, where by chance there is no water of Lake Mälaren, there are various old castles, like Skokloster, shall we say; it is a huge private building with an old park, but because there is a collection there, it is open to the public; on the other hand, right in front of the castle, about ten yards of lawn are shut off by a wire fence for the proprietor, one of the Brahe family, and provided with an inscription: *Private property*. Below, of course, is Lake Mälaren. Or there is the castle of Drottningholm, something like Versailles, but smaller; there are fountains standing in the park, and statues from the workshop of Adrian de Vries, which in times gone by, as people know, used to stand in our country, in the Wallenstein Palace; but, as you are aware, three hundred years ago the Swedes looted them from us, after which the Danes looted them from the Swedes, but they had to hand them back after a time; that's called history. Then there is a rococo theatre which was built by the lusty King Gustaf III, who acted in it, wrote plays and designed costumes; but it is common knowledge that we artists and writers seldom experience gratitude, and so King Gustaf was stabbed at a ball by some cavalier. In that theatre, to the present day, the decorations and theatrical equipment of the time has been preserved; the sea-wash in particular still functions faultlessly and even at the present day it creaks and groans as loudly as even most modern theatrical machines. And even now there are dressing-rooms for the performers, wardrobes, fittings, and original costumes, and it smells of dust, vanity, and mouldiness, like every theatre during the holidays; it is a wonder that it has kept so well. In the auditorium there is a throne, and rows of seats, in each row a label states for whom it is; for diplomats, ladies-in-waiting, chamberlains, officials, pages, and so on; in those days people were still sorted out one behind the other, and not right and left as in modern times. There are sheep grazing in the park, and in front of the castle, of course, is Lake Mälaren. Or there is a place called Sigtuna, where right away they have four ruined churches, a people's High School, and Lake Mälaren; once upon a time the royal seat used to be here, and there are lots of such-like places.

Uppsala: there is no Mälaren, but instead there is an old castle with fine oaken halls, and the Cathedral for the archbishop of Uppsala, where Linnaeus and Svedenborg sleep, and where Nathan Söderblom used to preach (turf now covers him, but even now I see him as he sat on a bank of thyme in Slovakia, and declared that some day people would come to their senses, and that there would be one church, one God, and one peace for all the world); and a famous University, with student colleges for thirteen "nations"—they are, in fact, the different districts of Sweden, but I hope that they behave like real cultured nations and carry among themselves conflicts, eternal hostility, and wars of life and death; then there is the University Library, and in it one of the rarest books in the world, the medieval Wulfila's Bible, Codex Argenteus, all written in silver on a purple parchment, and decorated with painted arcades and little pillars; that also used

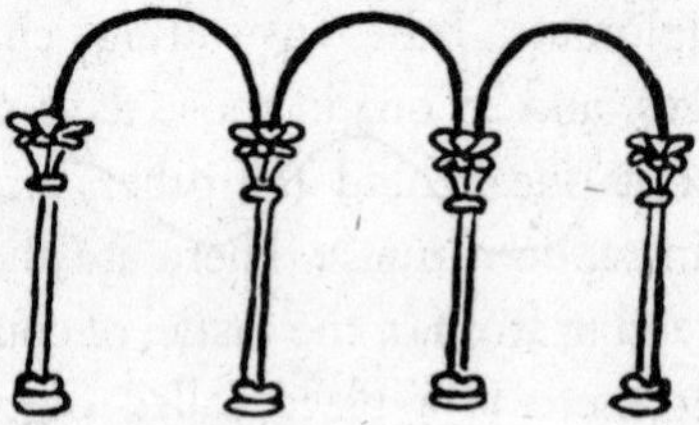

to be with us at Hradčany in the time of Rudolph, but the Swedes carried it off as desirable booty. And Great Scot, but here we begin to feel at home; here in the cases are papers from the hands of Banér, and Torstenson, Pappenheim, Wallenstein, Gustavus Adolphus, and Christian of Anhalt, and Bernhard of Weimar—all, should I say, countrymen at the time of the Thirty Years' War; such fine old acquaintances, such popular enemies; after all, it pleases you when you meet them abroad.

And a bit further away is Gamla Uppsala, the old Uppsala; in pagan times it used to be the seat of the Swedish kings, but to-day there is only an old-world restaurant where from cattle horns you drink mead simply called *mjöd*; on each horn is written in silver who drank from it—from my horn the Prince of Wales drank, and other personalities from the ruling houses; perhaps that is the reason why the mead goes so much to your head. In front of the hotel stand three "Royal Hills"; they are barrows from the sixth century, as high as a four-storied house; every visitor climbs up on to them, but then he clambers down

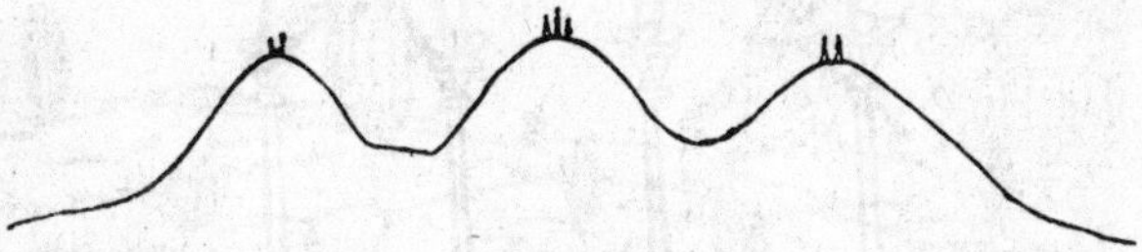

again because there's nothing on the top; for those centuries have been carried away into the Museum in Stockholm.

This now is Uppland, here around Uppsala; a country where Linnaeus used to collect and classify all the flowers of the earth; an attractive plain, nothing but pastures, nothing but meadows ringed by wooden fences, nothing but hay drying in long goat-like formations. And everywhere in that plain of fields and hay granite islands protrude, granite slabs and boulders, black granite mounds overgrown with ancient trees, and red farms; every farm here is built on a rock, like a burgh, perhaps so as not to use up one inch of living soil. Towards evening these farms burn with vermilion, like pods of paprica, in the moss-green of the meadows and orchards; here, there, scattered far and wide, each of them a little human island shining red in the vastness of space and time; I tell you, the world is beautiful.

And there are granite knolls on which perhaps some enchantment lies; and so no red house shines on them,

but they carry a ghastly windmill; or a clump of junipers, gnome-like and rather terrifying, has been planted on them; or a runic stone stands there in memory of some Harald, or Sigurd a thousand years ago. It is a sweet land, this Sweden; but haunted a bit in places.

* * * * *

You travel through Sweden past fields and woods; and from time to time you see a rough table standing by the roadside. What is it for? Well, somewhere from those solitudes the farmer puts churns here with milk from his herds; and from the town he is brought flour, or nails, and he comes here to fetch them when

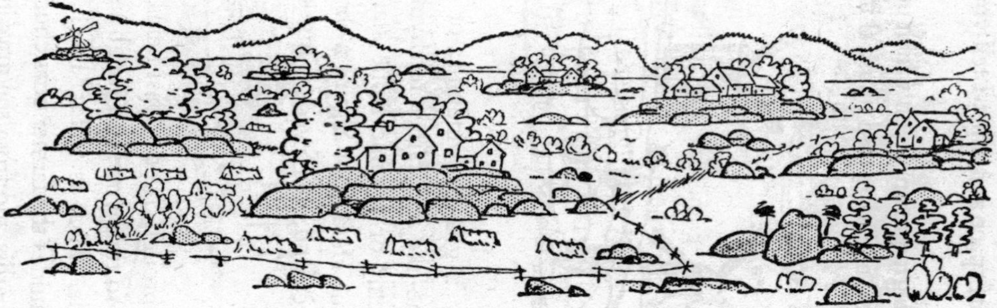

Uppland

he has time. Or in the middle of a wood a letter-box hangs on a post, or on a birch tree. Here the people

from the solitudes come for the letters which the postman leaves for them. Oh no, Sweden is not haunted; perhaps they have ghosts and gnomes here, and other rapscallions of that kind, but I should say that people trust one another here.

ON THE WAY

The route from Stockholm to Oslo consists chiefly of lakes; counting only from Laxå, there you have

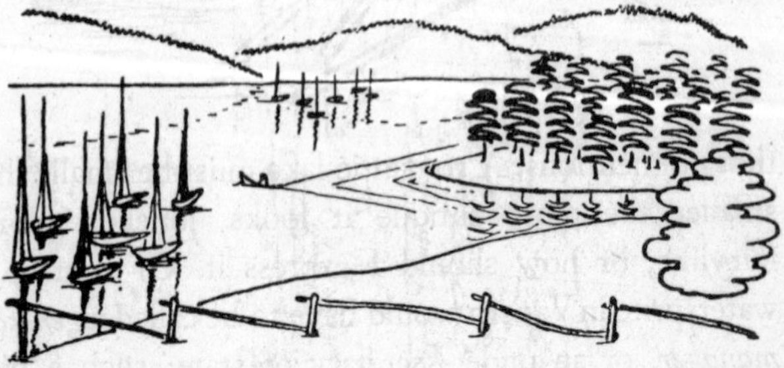

lakes Toften and Testen, then immense, flat Vänern, then Värmeln (this already is Värmland, the land of Gösta Berling), and Glafsfjorden, Nysorkensjön, and Bysjön. Strange: such a lake like Vänern, that is too big, has in it something fundamentally unromantic, and I should say almost modern; it must be

those dimensions. A romantic lake must be small; the smaller the more antique it looks, lonelier, more fairylike, or how should I express it. Of course, a watersprite in Vänern would have to be called a *general manager*, or an under-secretary of state; such a big concern it is, that Vänern. But there are also smooth lakes, like mirrors of heaven, and bottomless little lakes in the depths of the woods, and long, narrow river lakes, yes, and rivers, or *älvar*, slow, cutting into dark woods, and languidly, with a kind of eternity, bearing the trunks of felled trees; and the woods, observe how on the river slowly, endlessly, irresistibly the woods are flowing away.

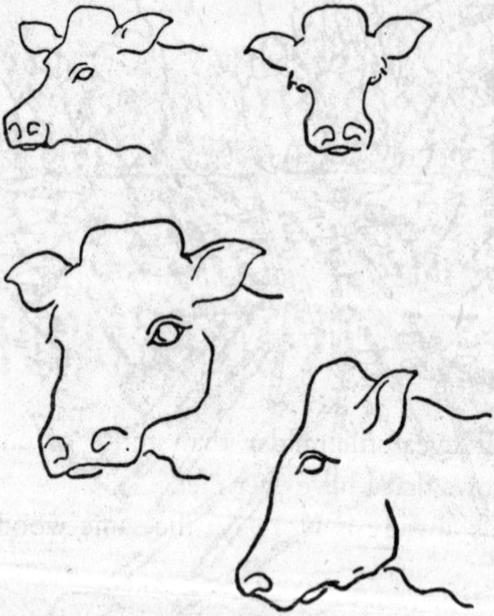

And then, after the *älver* and tunnels, comes Norway; and mountains and rocks; and hornless Norwegian cows. I have already seen the hairy Scotch cattle, and the huge, violet cattle of the Lake District, the black Spanish bulls, red and white little Alpine cows, white Magyar oxen, and Frisian cattle, dappled with black, like beans; but cows without horns I saw for the first time somewhere near Skotterud. They are small, brown, and bony; without those horns they look appealingly defenceless and almost embarrassed,

and their eyes still milder than those of any other sacred cows that I have ever met.

So this already is Norway: the same woods as on

the other side of the frontier, but rather more whipped with gales, and, instead of moss, littered with whitish lichen; the same lakes as on the other side, but rather sadder and more terrible, hewn between the rocks; the same mountains as on the other side of the frontier but higher, and steeper; similar valleys, but deeper; birches the same, but shaggier and stockier; granite the same, but rather heavier. Well, yes, mountains; that comes from being in the mountains here.

And wooden cottages the same as on the other side of the frontier, but poorer; and no longer are they

made of perpendicular planks, but of horizontal boards, and they are brown and grey like the rocks; and they do not stand any longer only just on the ground, but on stone, or on little wooden legs so that they do not get wet from below; and they are not covered with tiles, shingle, or thatch, but—with—what, in fact?—is it turf, or peat? Even now I don't really know, but it is thickly covered with moss, and grass, and willow-herb, nay even with real firs, and birches; the woods here also grow on men's roofs.

Everywhere here it oozes and exudes from under the round hillocks of grass and rushes; what is not rock is peat, everywhere they dig and dry the small

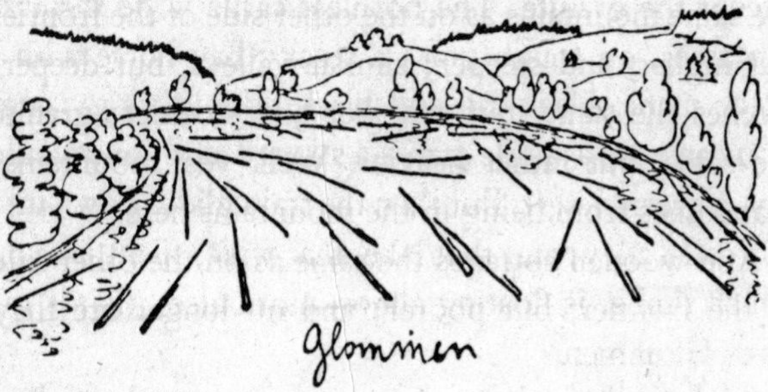
Glommen

piles of peat; men make their living from everything except the granite. The hornless cattle wade through morasses, on tough grass a stocky bay horse with a black mane, black tail and black nostrils, is grazing; you can't see a single man—a strange land; one would say, a green desert. But then the train glides down into a broad valley; and that lake, that wide, silent lake on which timber is floating almost motionless, that is the river Glommen.

And further along down Glommen, through a country of pastures, and men, under the pointed steeples of churches, past green slopes and valleys, past little red towns until it glistens with silver between the tops of the mountains: Oslofjord.

IV

Norway

IV

Norway

OSLO

From the look of things to-day a traveller ought first to enquire whether by chance some civil war, revolution, or congress is raging in the town for which he is making. We had hardly arrived in Stockholm before an International Congress of the Salvation Army broke out; groups of rather stiff, but healthy-looking gentlemen and elderly girls with straw hen-coops on their heads were chasing about in the streets searching for means to save you. And we set out on our retreat to Norway; but as soon as we entered Oslo, Sunday broke out, and on top of that a World Congress of Sunday School Teachers; you've no idea how many of them there are in the world. The whole of Oslo was inundated with some kind of virtuous swarming and twittering; every minute someone smiled at me with Christian patience, and asked me in English whether I was also going to Divine Service. At Karl Johans Gate it was not Ibsen's or Björnson's spirit that was stirring, but the spirit of the Anglo-Saxon Church Assembly; I was afraid that sullen Ibsen on his pedestal in front of the theatre might lift his head and also begin to preach on effective love towards one's neighbour, or something of that sort; but Ibsen didn't lift up his head, and altogether he looked as if he was annoyed about something; Björnson evidently bore it better. In Oslo I tried to find a solution to the problem: how it comes about that such a small, and as far as I was able to judge, a poor nation too, and that such a smallish, and as far as I could see, a rather ordinary town like Oslo, had given rise of themselves to such great and amazing literature. In the circumstances I did not find the solution; now marvel more than ever.

There was still another problem that pestered my mind; it also concerns literature, but chiefly language. Well, there aren't even three millions of those Norwegians; and yet they write in two or three languages of which not one is really quite alive. *Riksmål* is the town language, it is the old Danish, the historical, official, and literary language; *landsmål* is the old Norwegian and peasant language, but only in the south-western parts of the country, and beside that it has been artificially elaborated; as a matter of fact half a dozen different *landsmåls* are spoken, different ones in every valley; and there is a movement called *bymål* which desires to unite *riksmål* and *landsmål;* and a reform of spelling is suggested, according to which *riksmål* would be written in the *landsmål* way; in schools *landsmål* and *riksmål* are in use, depending on the wishes of the community; authors like Hamsun and Undset write in *riksmål*, or in *landsmål*, like Olaf Duun, or else differently too. You must admit that for a nation of three millions it is rather complicated, and it struck me that as concerns the language, in spite of all the fine Norwegian spirit of tolerance, this brave and strong little nation does not really feel quite at its ease. No doubt, in our case we have similar worries; but with us the question of language, or of dialect, is likely to take the form of a fundamental difference that is national and political. But for literature one lesson, I think, can be drawn from the linguistic situation in Norway; it should be written so that it is the mother tongue of a living race as it thinks and speaks in its time, and the language of the whole nation, of the élite, and of the people, of the town and of country. I know that it isn't easy, but that's why literature is called art, that it should work magic and do wonders, and increase in the desert the bread and fishes of experiences, words, and feelings; and if it is to speak to many, it must speak with very many words and dialects. And the flaming tongues of all the *landsmåls*, and of the old written monuments as well, and of all that has ever been written and spoken for these people will descend upon it; for it was for that reason that it was created, that through the words it should open all the treasures of the world, amen. And for this sermon the Sunday School teachers are responsible; for never in my life have I ever seen so much suppressed eloquence together, and proclivity to preach, as when four thousand of them were standing while only one of them was preaching. What can you do: you can't help it, and you begin to preach yourself, and instruct the others.

Nevertheless, thanks to the Divine Service already referred to, one could find a few places in Oslo where there were no Sunday School teachers at that time; up on Holmenkollen, for instance, where in winter people do ski-jumping, and from there one of the most beautiful views in the world can be seen: the long and meandering Oslofjord, with its islands and tiny steamers and mountain peaks, with its misty and silvery light; or a quiet row of villas, where behind a high fence lives Edvard Munch and lets no one come to him, so that you know that it is not only Hamsun who does it; and it is strange in the case of the great creators where so much bitterness towards people comes from. And in the Norwegian Museum, besides other things, I discovered a fine old picture in which John the Baptist christens Our Lord in a cold Norwegian fjord; it is a pity that they haven't got there the Flight from Egypt on skis as well; but on the other hand the native pictures of the Crucifixion show a peaceful and almost contented face—how far we are away here from the Catholic pathos of torment and death! Or, finally, there was one stark and almost holy place: a huge concrete shelter where the *Fram* reposes.

True, I also went to see the old Viking boats which

had been unearthed in the barrows. They are miraculously preserved and very beautiful in shape, and in a way the Norwegians come to pray to them. I am not exactly a seafarer, and I even look upon the trip across the Channel as a memorable adventure; but as I gazed at those black, savage, splendidly sprung Viking boats without a single iron rivet, I felt somewhere, right at the uttermost depths of my landsman's soul, that after all the sea is essentially a manly affair, even manlier than politics or the reformation of the world. To sit down in that black, arrogant Oseberg hull, and to set out into a sea of darkness and mist: don't you see, my girl, what fine fellows we are, we men!—Well, true, I went to see it and to pay homage; but what is it compared with the *Fram*!

You couldn't even expect it of her; such an ordinary, smallish boat she is, of solid wood it's true, and with her beams stiffened a bit with props and girders so that she could withstand something; the little kitchen like the palm of your hand, the engine-room something to laugh at, the stairs and doors so that anybody could knock his head against them; and then a little cabin as if for a child, and on it is written *Sverdrup;* and another one with a trestle bed, on which even our Fráňa Šrámek couldn't stretch his legs, and on it is written *Nansen*; and then the third cabin, still a bit shorter, and above it the notice *Amundsen.* And in every one of these little boxes of planks, on a spiked nail is a fur cap, and shoes of seal-skin; it smells of naphthaline and of sadness here. And then the sextant used by Nansen, Sverdrup, Amundsen, and the telescope, and the other things whatever names these navigation instruments possess; and dental forceps; surgical scissors, scalpels, bandages, a tiny dressing outfit—there is nothing else there. So praise to God, and blessing: here we are at home again, in the home of our boyhood. Do you remember Nansen and Sverdrup? Do you remember how you spent the winter in the *Fram*? It was in daddy's garden, syringas and roses were in flower there; we shot a polar bear, and we set out with dogs and sledges over the snowfields toward the North; but bad weather, and the state of the ice forced us to turn back. It was a wearisome return, yet remember; it's of no avail, we must get back before the polar night sets in. AT LAST OUR *Fram* APPEARED ON THE HORIZON AND WE GREETED HER WITH CHEERS.—Yes, our *Fram*; for it belonged to us all, the boys who read in the world; let it be, this is OUR boat, and we have the right to touch with reverence, and intimacy, any sextant, coil of rope or dental forceps. Only here on this little cabin is written Amundsen; that then is already another chapter, which we read at another time, and in a different way; here we do not touch anything with a childish finger, but we take off a man's hat. (For it is close here, or is it the naphthaline that does it.) Well then, here the man slept whose name was Amundsen; if so he had to draw his legs up very much when he was sleeping here.

The man who saw both poles. The man who lost himself when he flew into such a wilderness to save someone who unnecessarily and ostentatiously had interfered with HIS Arctic. This, of course, is another adventure still more deeply inscribed than the reminiscences from the books of childhood.

* * * * *

…vening, late in the evening, there were …hool teachers any more, but a light …t; on Karl Johans Gate Ibsen's spirit …stily, and the people at home enjoyed … Sunday; the crowd is somewhat more …red than over there in Sweden, more …ectable, and altogether more like people; … elated, like nations that have an inclina… …rink, and politics; and as far as one can … faces, one need not be afraid of them.

BERGENSBANEN

The Bergen mountain railway belongs to the so-called wonders of engineering. Wonders of engineering, as a rule, are tunnels and viaducts; but the Bergen railway has this peculiarity that the tunnels, should I say, are artificial ones, built over the ground, constructed of posts and boards. These tunnels here simply guard against avalanches and the snow-drifts, and they extend for miles and miles of the journey, chiefly in the most interesting places; and where there are no tunnels at any rate there are high wooden fences; but nevertheless here and there the patient sightseer finds a spot where the carpenter has left a hole, and for a while he can feel amazed at the beauty and sublimity of the world while he is going through

the next wooden tunnel. But to take things in their proper order, this marvel of engineering does not begin until Ustedal, and along the Ustakveikja; at first the train runs along, partly through ordinary tunnels in the ground, partly through green Norway, through woods and pastures, beside the rivers and lakes; and all the time there is something to look at, the wooden farmhouses and polled cattle, the hills and dales, until Hønefoss arrives, famous for its waterfall and Trotsky in exile, and then the sweet valley of Sokna, comely and fresh pastures between dark forests, and everywhere scattered over the green slopes little brown houses of wood, standing on legs like the castle of Baba Yaga—

The man who saw both poles. The man who lost himself when he flew into such a wilderness to save someone who unnecessarily and ostentatiously had interfered with HIS Arctic. This, of course, is another adventure still more deeply inscribed than the reminiscences from the books of childhood.

* * * * *

And in the evening, late in the evening, there were no Sunday School teachers any more, but a light northern night; on Karl Johans Gate Ibsen's spirit blew rather frostily, and the people at home enjoyed their summer Sunday; the crowd is somewhat more broad-shouldered than over there in Sweden, more rural, less respectable, and altogether more like people; it looks rather elated, like nations that have an inclination towards drink, and politics; and as far as one can judge by their faces, one need not be afraid of them.

BERGENSBANEN

The Bergen mountain railway belongs to the so-called wonders of engineering. Wonders of engineering, as a rule, are tunnels and viaducts; but the Bergen railway has this peculiarity that the tunnels, should I say, are artificial ones, built over the ground, constructed of posts and boards. These tunnels here simply guard against avalanches and the snow-drifts, and they extend for miles and miles of the journey, chiefly in the most interesting places; and where there are no tunnels at any rate there are high wooden fences; but nevertheless here and there the patient sightseer finds a spot where the carpenter has left a hole, and for a while he can feel amazed at the beauty and sublimity of the world while he is going through

the next wooden tunnel. But to take things in their proper order, this marvel of engineering does not begin until Ustedal, and along the Ustakveikja; at first the train runs along, partly through ordinary tunnels in the ground, partly through green Norway, through woods and pastures, beside the rivers and lakes; and all the time there is something to look at, the wooden farmhouses and polled cattle, the hills and dales, until Hønefoss arrives, famous for its waterfall and Trotsky in exile, and then the sweet valley of Sokna, comely and fresh pastures between dark forests, and everywhere scattered over the green slopes little brown houses of wood, standing on legs like the castle of Baba Yaga—

wrinkled, bent, broken, or cut; the fashioning in granite was terrible; one speaks of geological ages, but what amount of work do they reveal! Never mind, the Ice Age, that was a dreadful workshop; just see what craftsmanship there was then, and what marvels in

technique there are! And the man who has no understanding of stone knows little of the beauty and great majesty of the world.

And then comes Hallingdal, an old farming valley, famous for its peasant art; here at one time the famous Hallingdal roses were painted, and even to the present day one can see with what loving skill the local people constructed their stockade farms out of beams as strong as thunder, their hay-lofts set out broadly on narrow pedestals of timber, their antique churches like towers, resembling wooden pagodas, their carved windows, gables and pillars—all beautiful, thorough, antique work of solid beams and boards; and those who have no appreciation of wood will miss much of the pithy, resiny, and peasant beauty of the world.

Yes, wood and stone, that is Hallingdal. And forests, forests of nothing but masts: such kind of tall

Hallingdal

trees they are. And hay on very long racks, herds of small brown cows, thick-set ponies with black manes, all meadows, all silky grass, yellow camomile and white meadow-sweet, the blue of the campanulas as in no other place, vermilion geraniums in the wooden windows, that is Hallingdal.

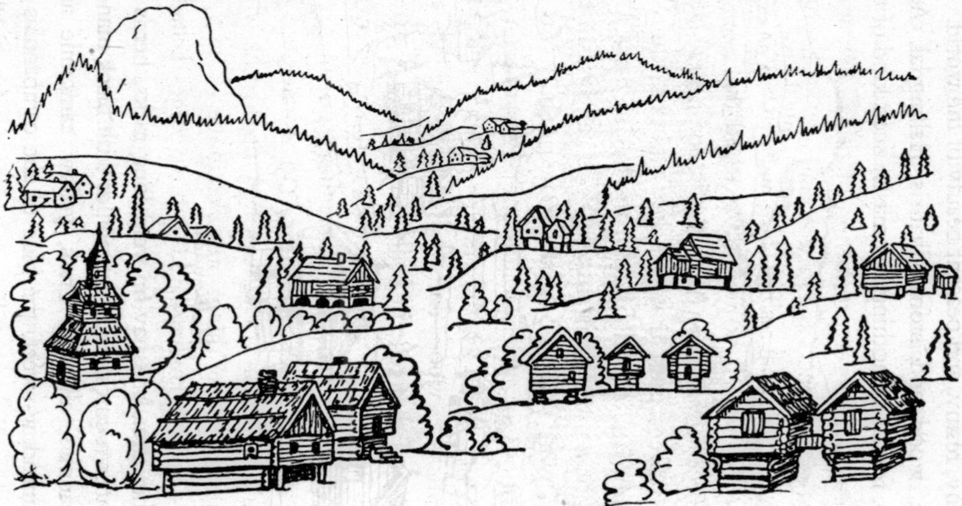

Hallingdal

It is strange that perhaps all over the world the peasant habit to carve, paint, and embroider has chiefly developed particularly in mountainous countries. I know, it is partly because in isolated valleys a comparatively larger proportion of things belonging to great-grandfathers and great-grandmothers has been preserved; but that which has been preserved had first to originate. I think it's the wood that does it; put a piece of wood in a boy's hands, and he will begin (for it's a certainty that he's got a pocket knife) to carve notches, and clefts until the hilt of a sword, a statue, or a pillar takes shape. Wood can be cut, and painted with colours, while stone is only fit for fortifications, or ancient tombstones. Peasant art, from architecture down to the shepherd's pipe and bagpipes, sticks to wood; and so it sticks to the hills and woods; and therefore in Hallingdal the heart of man rejoices in the same way as it does in the Pyrenees, in the Alps, or in our country, where the mountains grow. Stony are the works of Nature, and wooden are the fashionings of man; or at least they used to be while the natural order of things prevailed in the world.

This then is Hallingdal; but now comes Ustadal, and that already is quite another world; here now nobody lives but stationmasters, and the personnel of the mountain hostels; everything else is rock, and cold lakes, and quagmires in eruption; still the battered pine holds out, and the dwarfed, crooked birch, or crouching alder; only here and there a palisade hut with

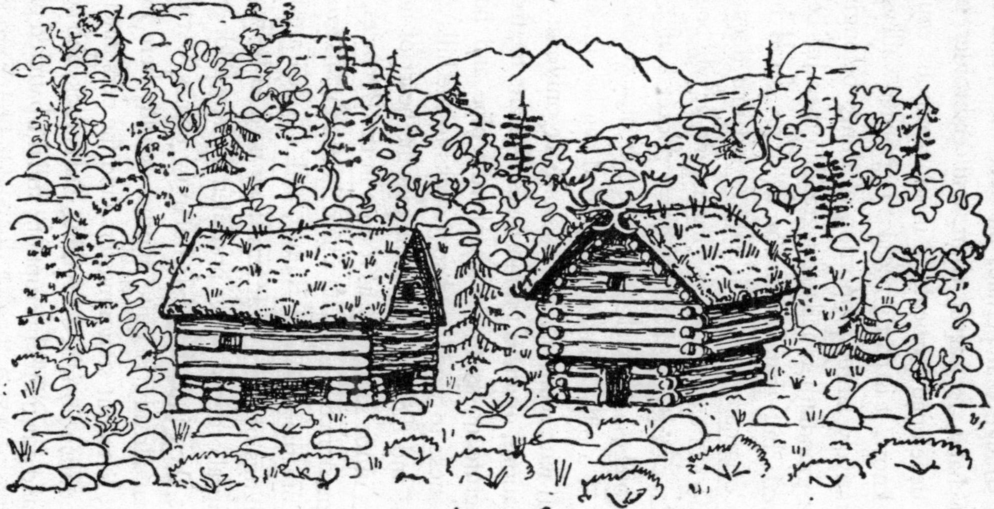

Ustadal

reindeer antlers on the gable; and then nothing more but stones and creeping birch, rush and cotton-grass;

and then not even rocks, or lakes, or vegetation, but only wooden tunnels, galleries and barriers against the snow-drifts; so strange a country it is.

Finsedal

And then already we are quite high up, at Finse; it is only four thousand feet above sea level, but in the local conditions of the North it is as if it were ten thousand feet high with us. The end of life. Lakes which do not even thaw in summer; it might not be worth their while. Tongues of eternal glaciers reaching

Finsevatn

to the railway, the white firn field, Hardangerjøkelen, snow drifts along the railway; this then they call July.

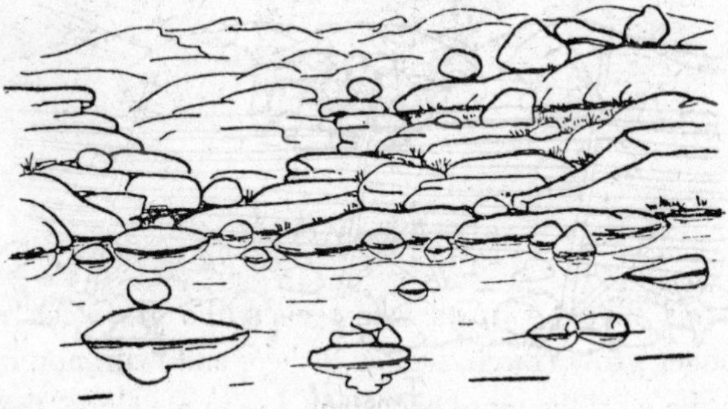

Tangevatn

Here and there men wait beside the railway to greet something living when the train passes by. Snow fields, steely grey lakes and stony ruins; a pinch of brown grass, and that's all; perhaps it is so massive and tremendous because there is no life now.

There is no life now, but still man subsists there; man is as tough as that creeping arctic willow which

Raundal

forms silvery carpets where even the grass can no longer grow. Birch, willow, lichen, and man: nothing in the world is more persistent. Leave me alone, there is something I must do here; I have to wave with both hands to those who are living here. And to other men of other countries as well; in all places in the world man has to suffer much, but here the only things against him are those eternal elements. God bless you, men from Ustakveikja, fare you well, men from Moldådal; it is nice for you here, you live your hard life here in comfort, is it any concern of yours that somewhere else history is being made?

So remember me at home, goodbye, I must hurry, for we are going downhill; down between the rocks, down from above Flåmsdal and its waterfalls, down

to the woods and pine trees, down to Raundal where again the farmer with a queer short scythe is gathering his hay, between the granite boulders; down among men and solitary dwellings—time goes fast when you travel downhill! And here again thrives the Nordic profusion of trees: pines as tall as towers, or like blackberries up to your knees, and ferns up to your waist; and a couple of waterfalls; further down, spruces again and firs like cathedrals; and several cascades lower down, already we are among the billowy growth of the mountain ashes, alders, willows, and aspens; the frontiers of vegetation are so near together and so well defined that one wonders how Nature here in Norway sticks so closely to the ecological and biological laws of plant life; that must be due to general education.

By now we are quite low down, only twenty or

thirty feet above the sea; low down, beside beautiful lakes among the leafy groves by the red farms and clear meadows; everywhere higher up granite cupolas with white belts of eternal snow—well, it is very nice; only one would like to know what it looks like on the other side of the mountains. And here that narrow green lake, that already is a fjord of the sea: perpendicular rocks and between them a strip of calm and bottomless water; it is bewitchingly sad, and terribly intimate; only except that at first it seems completely unreal. It needs time to get used to the fjords, before you can begin to accept them as stark and even hard reality. Over there a bit higher up, I mean in Sognefjord, through the day the people have to tether

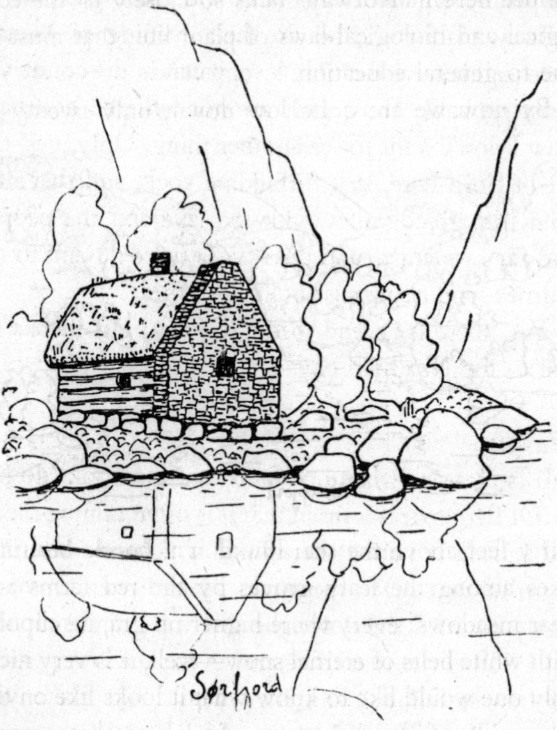

their children so that they cannot fall from those perpendicular walls into the sea. You can't believe the different places where people live.

Thank goodness Bergen is coming at last; it is strange what an effort it is to keep looking. Just shut your eyes, and see nothing; only that rock there, and the fisherman's hut, and nothing more; good night, and I don't care a damn. Only, yes, a couple of those perpendicular mountains still; and those girls on the railway platform, who do their evening promenade here as if it were the only level patch in the country—most probably those girls are not tethered here; and now I don't want to see another thing. Only, yes, this bit of fjord here, that forbidding rock, and that's all. And that green valley with the lake and the people, and the mountains and the sky. Is there no end to the journey, and to gazing about?

Yes, there is an end to the journey; but there's no end to the Northern day.

BERGEN

It is pleasant when one finds that the books do not lie. Of Bergen it is written that it is often raining there; and indeed it rained there until it poured. And it is recorded that seven mountain peaks tower above it; I only counted three, for the rest were in the clouds, but I do believe that there are seven; the Norwegians are honest fellows, and they would not make you believe what is not holy truth.

Therefore I certify that Bergen is an old and glorious Hansa town; of that Hansa the German embankment, or Tyskebrygge, with little old wooden houses still remains; and the Hansa Museum where one may find preserved the chests in which the Hansa

Tyskebrygge

merchants used to lock their apprentices and clerks up for the night so that they would not wander about, and so that they would not catch cold; and old mer-

Tyskekirken

chant houses, warped like a concertina with protruding gables into which goods were hauled with pulleys straight from the boats.

And then there is a fish-market smelling of ancient fishiness, and full of blue and silver fish; and old alleys of wooden, whitewashed, terribly dear little houses; but many of these have already been burnt down, and because of that Bergen as a whole looks like a modern and prosperous town. And there is an old church, Tyskekirken, where you pay an entrance fee; but it is worth it, for inside there is a fine Gothic altar, and old votive pictures representing numerous and well-fed merchant families; and on the top of that there is a wedding taking place, a carroty sailor is marrying a freckled lass who weeps virgin-like while a young pastor splices them, and he looks like a record holder at ski-jumping; also there are relations, some of them in silk, some in dinner jackets with white ties, moved and solemn, shedding tears; and thus inadvertently one gets one's money worth.

And besides there is Håkon's Coronation Hall in Bergen, and Rosenkrantz' Tower; and directly below them the boat is anchored which is going to take us to Trondheim. Hello, little boat; here we are.

AS FAR AS NIDAROS

True enough, it was a nice boat; it was a brand new mail-boat with all the comforts that a modest human heart could desire; the only unfortunate thing was the cargo which that boat was taking to the North. By this I don't mean cabbages, flour, and such-like things which we took on board below Bergenhus; but it was a worse business with the spiritual cargo, which consisted of a collective gathering of some American church, or Christian society, which was on an expedition somewhere to Nordkapp; I didn't dare to ask who they really were, fearing that they might have converted me to their faith.

So I do not know what is the doctrine of that American Church; as far as one could ascertain, well:

1. With hearty to-do it throws rope rings onto pegs, or chases round the deck some kind of wooden disc which gets under the feet of the other travellers,

in which way that holy community captured victoriously and completely the whole prow of the boat even before we had weighed anchor;

2. with overwhelming sociability and breeziness they open conversations on the one side among themselves, on the other with the other passengers; in consequence of which, at one stroke, they mastered the entire stern of the boat with all the seats and deck-chairs, which by the way they immediately covered with their shawls, novels, bibles and bags as a sign of their permanent usage and prescriptive ownership;

3. at table they sing bellicose Christian songs so that they oust the rest of us, unorganized, and weak minority, also from the ship's dining-room;

4. they organize nothing but social games, dances, community singing, devotions, and other pastimes; most probably they are practising some joyful Christianity and spreading relentlessly round them the innocent jollity of the spirit that is pleasing to God; I tell you, it was frightful;

5. they give effect zealously to effective love towards their neighbours, taking care of people afflicted by sea-sickness, of dogs, of the newly married, of children, sailors, natives, and foreigners too, chiefly by addressing them, and encouraging them, by shouting heartily to them, greeting them, and smiling at them, and altogether menacing them with sheer kindness; and so there was nothing left for the rest of us to do but to barricade ourselves in the cabins, and curse there in sullen silence. God be merciful to our souls!

* * * * *

Why, it is beautiful here; just look, that quiet and clear fjord among the rocks of Nord-Hordland, and the granite shores of the islands; just look, that sunset splashed with pink and moisture over the whole sky, over the vast sea, between the hills which are becoming a misty indigo blue; and that fishing boat which passes us ghost-like with its little red light—Lord, how beautiful it is! And the holy community began in that divine evening to bleat a hymn.

It seems that it accepts as its members ladies chiefly

of a certain age; truth to tell they were rather like warriors, except for a few frail, drowsing, more or less centenarian grannies; besides one imp of sixty

years wearing a skirt above her knees and a child's hat, one lady with a horsey face, one with a rash, and one without any obvious physical defect; a batch of widows of various ages from dyed hair to silver grey;

Nord-Hordland

one gentleman with squirrel's teeth, and one oldish dapper little fellow not unlike a dried kipper, and suffering presumably from liver; a group of elderly girls on the whole bravely bearing their lot; in short, it looked like an ordinary charitable organization, but there ought not to be so many of them together; it is simply disturbing. And they ought not to sing to the honour and glory of the Creator. Or at least not here. If someone said to them, look at His work and glory, and keep your mouths shut—

Then the congregation stopped singing, and gazed around. The lady with the horsey face put on her pince-nez. "Isn't it nice?"

"Wonderful!"

"And what shall we play next?"

Simply irrepressible; it is amazing what strength faith gives to human souls!

* * * * *

It can't go on any longer like this; let us throw these American saints into the sea; or at least let us go and blaspheme those wooden discs what they push over the deck; I know it is a great sin, but at least there will be some fun! And let's have a drink so that the evil spirit of revolt descends upon us; and then making a clean breast of it, and tightening our belts, we will kick their discs, and scatter their rings: Go to sleep, you saints! There are people here who have something to settle with the evening, the sea, sky, silence, and so on; look out, clear off, or something will happen.

But nothing happened because there is no alcohol for sale on Norwegian boats.

* * * * *

It was a miracle, it seems. The American saints were just about to start another hymn, and their spiritual shepherd—he was a fattish agent of salvation, who prattled like a barber, and as a badge of his spiritual office he wore a ding-donging little cross about the place where ordinary people have their kidneys—well then, this spiritual shepherd blew a whistle, and then the most bulky saint clambered on to the platform, sat down on the box with the loud speaker, closed her eyes, and opened her mouth ready to chant; that very moment, beneath her skirts, a rattling and intensely secular foxtrot broke out. The venerable lady sprang up as if she had sat down on a red-hot oven, but the spiritual shepherd showed what a great man he was; he simply pushed the tuning-fork into his trousers pocket, and clapped his hands. "Well, let's dance!" and he took the lady with the rash for his partner.

* * * * *

Morning on the open sea; we must be sailing round the point of Stattland; here in the open Sildegapet it is always a bit rough. You can see it at once; a couple of people on deck are sick with animation and without effort, while the others are in desperate difficulties. The congregation stayed down below; most likely to pray.

But see if it isn't beautiful: the grey sea with the white crests of the waves; and on the right the bare, notchy, brawny shore of Norway; and the seagulls screaming as they float on the long crests of the breeze. You can peer down into the water churned up by the keel; it is green like sulphate of iron, like malachite, like an iceberg, or something; and with a fierce scum of white, lined with trimmings of foam, look, the track behind us marked out by foam right to the horizon; and see how it tosses about that fishing smack, a man is standing on it, and he waves at our boat with paws like a polar bear—

"Hello," hollers the spiritual shepherd, and waves his cap in return; clearly he does it in the name of his Church, of the United States, and of the Christian world as a whole.

* * * * *

Again it is a fjord clasped by rocks on both sides; the water has quietened down, it is lovely, smooth, and shining; the congregation is coming up the deck and distributing smiles. "A fine day!" "How beautiful!" "Wonderful, isn't it?" The little flock have wrapped themselves up in rugs and occupied all the seats; after that they put on their spectacles and begin to read novels and other holy books,chattering zealously about their friends in America. The spiritual shepherd takes a turn round them, breezily slaps the grannies and shouts heartily; altogether it looks as if he had taken charge of the boat. What can we do, we are all at the mercy of his humanitarian activity; that fellow will save us yet if we do not forcibly put him out on a desert island. I would like to join in with a couple of men in whom I have faith; one Norwegian, who has just married a poor, pretty, lame girl; one gentleman who looks like an Italian count, and travels with a fine-looking dark lady; one crook who wears a Texas hat and a khaki shirt, for ever sitting with his beer, and telling people about his adventures with cowboys, gold-miners, or fur-trappers; in short, we should be enough for the job only we can't get together because on the boat we can't get anything respectable to drink. *Ikke alkohol*, that's the pity.

* * * * *

At last the boat ties up in Ålesund; it is a biggish harbour smelling of fish all right. The American shepherd organizes an invasion of his flock into Ålesund; and we others, we will have a look to see what we can buy. Yes, in every other shop they are selling very promising bottles on which it is written that it is rum, or pineapple, or punch extract; but they have no alcohol? *Ikke alkohol*, they say, waving their arms about. What, *ikke alkohol?* And what then do the brave sailors drink here? *Ikke alkohol*, they repeat, and shrug their shoulders with regret. A strange town, that Ålesund.

All right, keep it; but we shall go to Molde. Molde is a town of flowers they say; it would be something if you couldn't find there anything to buy! Well then,

Molde; a nice town, and there they have, on the other side of Romsdalsfjord, beautiful pointed mountains; and gardens full of roses and aqualegias; and a wooden church, but there the American shepherd had already penetrated, and begun to preach. A town of flowers, yes; but *ikke alkohol.* Sorry, says the shop-keeper, but you can't get any alcohol here; there is no *vinmonopolet* here.

All right, keep it; but we shan't go back to the boat now, let the American Church rage there as much as it likes; for all I care let them convert to their faith the captain, or the styrman, together with the crew; we shall go over the mountains here to Gjemnes, and we shall embark there for somewhere again. The car had already hooted, rattled, and suddenly it stopped; into the carriage the spiritual shepherd with three little sheep pushed his way, and he sat down more or less in our laps. "And now we can start," he announced heartily; after this he began to shout to the children in Molde, the town of flowers: "Hello, hello! Do you speak English? No! And you over there, you know English? No? Well, say something, boy! Don't you know English?" The Apostle from Massachusetts can't even grasp that, and he turns to me: "But you speak English, yes? No? And where do you come from? Prague? Yes, Prague. I was in Prague. Very nice. A very nice town."

"Wonderful."

There we were driving along the Romsdal riviera,

along Fannefjord; a beautiful spot, the blue fjord, mountains like the Alps; God, I should like to look at it, but the shepherd wriggles all the time, and bends over his little flock. Everywhere here there are farms

Fannefjord

for silver foxes, and the fishermen dry cod on the very walls of their cottages; I haven't seen it yet; it must be a hard life when one realizes what a smell cod like that makes. In the meantime the shepherd airs his views on the education of children, or something; the little sheep nod their heads, and with admiration pipe their yes, indeed, and how true; then the spiritual leader bangs his head against the top of the car, and loses his speech; and he looks through the window at the granite mountains:

"Lovely, isn't it?"

"Wonderful!"

"Well, what have we been talking about—"

We go on through wood and dale, over a rainy plain, sad like the end of the world, underneath the snow of the mountains, past the fishing hamlets; meanwhile the indefatigable shepherd gurgles about what Mrs. James ought not to do. How true! Yes. Indeed. And this sad water may be Tingvollfjord, and that cheerful water, that may be Batnfjord; and the spiritual adviser discourses on angina, cancer, and other cases; they are all moral diseases, he asserts; only moral, yes. Yes. Right. Isn't it?

Gjemnes at last, a tiny harbour like the palm of your hand, three men are waiting here for the motorboat to Kristiansund; higher up snow on the green cupolas of the mountains, down below green water full of brown seaweed; it is like a golden faded pattern on green brocade. "Do you speak English?" booms the spiritual shepherd, gathering round him the three who are waiting; they don't understand him, and they find themselves in the agony of embarrassment, but that doesn't worry him; he slaps them on the back and goes on talking cheerfully. A goodhearted fellow, no doubt about that.

And then the motorboat comes which takes people round about the fjord. The Apostle embarks his flock, and now he looks for someone to talk to. The flock secures everything on which it is possible to sit, and they begin to chatter incessantly; while round about is a fine fjord, and it is nearly evening; the mountains are steaming with the vapour from the rain which has fallen before, a rainbow vaults itself, the water turns to gold, and like silk it mirrors the bluish rocks; from below comes the throb of the boat's screw, and the

breezy voice of the shepherd. Strange, here inside the fjord everything is so blessed and green like a garden; the nearer the sea, the barer the rocks, till there is nothing but the bare stone, here and there a fisherman's hut and some large troughs on the grey boulders; they must be for salting the cod. No tree anywhere, only brown tufts of grass between the boulders; here the earth provides nothing for man but rock on which to dry his fish.

"Nice weather, eh, isn't it?" proclaims the shepherd.

"Yes, lovely."

"Wonderful."

* * * * *

And this is Kristiansund, the metropolis of cod fishing, if you care to know; a wooden town, all business houses, all gables for storage; grey, green, red little houses, clustered round the harbour; and on the crest of every roof nothing but gulls, in all my life I have never seen so many sea-gulls; perhaps they perform here some spiritual exercise.

Well, then, we must go back to our boat; but we have picked up an appendix, we shall carry football players from Kristiansund to a match with Trondheim; the whole town accompanies the heroes to the boat. Even the local dogs come running and wag their tails with glee. The spiritual shepherd beams, for he likes a crowd; he leans with his tummy over the rails and with friendly shouts he pesters the local dogs. What can such a dog do? He hangs his tail and disappears. And then that great man breezily addresses the local populace. "Do you speak English? Yes? No? Nice weather, what? Ha, ha, ha."

The screw churns, the boat sets out from the harbour; all the people in Kristiansund wave their hats and cheer their local heroes with triple shouts, or something.

The spiritual shepherd swings his cap, and thanks Kristiansund for its homage in the name of America and of the whole civilized world.

* * * * *

Kristiansund

Please tell me, styrman, where in Norway can you get a drop of alcohol? Suppose, if you need it to wash down rancour, drown a worm, drink for courage, or so on; can nothing be done?

Nothing, sir; the coast is sacred here. From Bergen as far as Trondheim *ikke alkohol.* Not till Trondheim is there a *vinmonopolet*, then in Bodö, Narvik, and Tromsø; there you can get anything you like to buy. But not here, said the styrman sadly; only holy people live here. In our country it is true there is a state monopoly, but each town can vote for itself whether the *vinmonopolet* is allowed to sell there or not. They used to drink here, sir, the styrman waved his hand. But in Trondheim, it's good there.

In Trondheim* we escaped at night from that boat. As I say, she was a good, new boat; but the whole misfortune was the cargo which she carried.

* Trondheim, originally Nidaros, later Trondheim, after the abolition of the union with Sweden again Nidaros, but now either Trondhjem, or Trondheim, according to whether you are talking landsmål, or riksmål; a considerable town, and rich, with an old harbour on the river Nid, with two * main streets, which are called Munkegate and Kongensgate, a royal seat called Stiftsgard, which is, they say, the largest wooden building in Norway, a famous ** cathedral, and a *** vinmonopolet (right by the harbour so that you won't miss it). The vinmonopolet is open from eleven a.m. till five p.m., whereas the Nidaros minster only opens its doors from twelve a.m. till two p.m. Here (that is in the cathedral) the heroine of Mrs. Sigrid Undset, Kristin, the daughter of Lavran, made a pilgrimage; to the present day it is a beautiful cathedral, although restored with piety. Besides that there is a big Freemasons' house, but that is found in all the larger Northern towns. A flourishing business with fish, wood, and English detective stories.

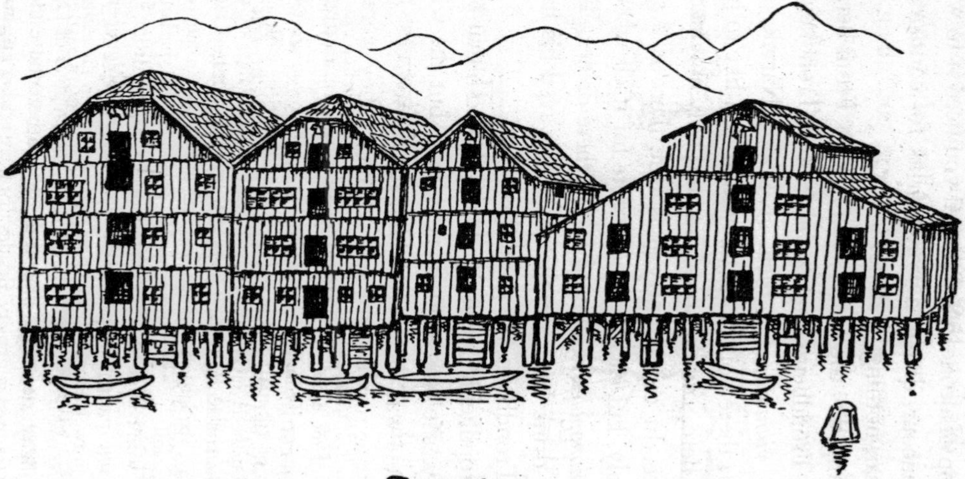

Trondheim

ON BOARD THE "HÅKON ADALSTEIN"

I give this boat her full name, first because she deserves it, and then because most likely she won't ever carry any passengers again; this year, poor thing, she served as a transport for people for the last time. She will lose her smoking-saloon, and her little cabins, and

she will only carry coal to Svolvær, or Hammerfest; things are so transitory.

To tell the truth the first impressions from the mole at Trondheim were not very exciting; they were just loading the *Håkon* with bricks; the crane made a horrible rattle; and the boat, I saw, was somehow amazingly small, smaller than the *Primator Dittrich*, with us on the Vltava. Does one go to North Cape in such a small boat?

On those bricks stood a huge, fat, terribly sweet gentleman with his hands in his pockets. "Mr. Captain," said an anxious soul who accompanies me on my way through life, and on the voyage north. "Mr. Captain, the boat is rather small, isn't she?"

The captain beamed, "Jaaa," he gurgled with appreciation. "Quite a small boat, ma'am. Very comfortable."

Comfortable, that's true; they are just loading her with sacks of cement. "And Mr. Captain, isn't the boat rather old?"

"Ne-e-ei," reassures the captain. "Quite a new boat. Entirely refitted."

"And when was she refitted?"

The captain pondered for a while. "Nineteen hundred and two," he said. "She's a fine boat."

"And how old is she altogether?"

"Ja," the captain drew in his breath. "Sixty-two years, ma'am."

The anxious terrestrial soul merely blinked. "And so, can she carry all those bricks and that cement? Won't she sink?"

"Ne-e-ei," asserted the captain. "We are still going to take three hundred sacks of flour."

"And all these cases as well?"

"Jaa. We shall take everything," the captain soothed the soul in distress. "And we have still to take on two hundred tons of ballast. Ja."

"Why?"

"So that the boat doesn't capsize, ma'am."

"And might she capsize?"

"Neei."

"And could she run into another ship?"

"Neei. Unless there's fog."

"And is it often foggy here in the summer?"

"O ja. Fog, that may come sometimes. Jaa." The captain blinks his friendly blue eyes under the long brushes of his eyebrows; I think that he wears those brushes so as not to have to shield his eyes with his hand when he is looking out for some rock.

"The boat only sails in the summer, doesn't she?"

"Neei. In winter as well. Every fortnight, there and back."

"And how many days are you at home?"

"Two days. Fifty days in a year."

"That's dreadful," worries the compassionate soul. "Fifty days! And aren't you lonely?"

"Neei. It's quite nice. Ja. In winter, then we have no passengers; then sometimes there's ice on the deck so thick that it has to be chopped off all the time. Ja."

"So that it is not so slippery?"

"Neei. So that the boat doesn't sink. Ja," the captain sighed contentedly. "A very fine boat. You'll want to stay on her."

* * * * *

Captain, I beg to announce that we should like to stay on her; it is really quite cosy here; the decks like the palm of your hand, a couple of wicker chairs, and that's all, no humbug; the smoking-saloon of green plush, something between a brothel of the eighties and a first-class waiting-room at a rural station; *spisesael* of red plush, and a dozen cabins with appurtenances—two berths looking like ironing-boards, two lifebelts called *livbelt*, and two spitoons for seasickness. You can't sit on those ironing-boards, they have an iron rail so that you don't fall off when the boat rocks; the pillow is as skimpy as a child's nappie, but instead, you make use of your lifebelt, and then it's all right. Instead of conceited stewards, a bandy-legged woman and a cross-tempered old girl; you just feel at home here.

Right over your head the winch rattles; it's a bit disturbing at first, but you get used to it; at any rate you know what's going on in the boat. There is a different rattle when they are loading flour, and another one when it is bricks; you wouldn't believe how much can be stored in a boat like this.

Midnight, and the *Håkon Adalstein* is still loading bags and cases in the harbour at Trondheim; she has already hooted for the second and third time; she begins to boil near the screws. The *Håkon* shook, creaked, and began to move. Well, a happy journey,

and good night; not until now has it felt like a journey north.

* * * * *

"Get up! Listen, get up!"

"What is it?"

"But water's coming in here!"

"But it isn't."

"It is! It's splashing through the port-hole!"

"Um."

"What?"

"Nothing. I said um."

"Well, I want you to do something!"

"Why?"

"Because the water's coming in here! We shall sink!"

"Um."

"For God's sake don't go to sleep and—"

"I'm not." The husband sits up and fumbles for the switch. What is it?"

"The water's coming in here! Through the port-hole!"

"Through the port-hole. Um. It must be shut, that's all."

"Well, shut it, and don't say um."

"Um." The husband lifts himself up from the ironing-board, climbs over the rail, and goes to shut the port-hole. Outside it is clear daylight, and the open sea with little white crests on the waves—sea, *ikke* fjord! that's why it's a bit—

"Eh, by jove," murmurs the husband.

"What is it?"

"But it is splashing in here through the porthole!"

"Well shut the port-hole, that's all."

The husband curses under his breath, and tries to shut the port-hole; but for those screws one ought to have a French key.

"Oh, blast it!"

"What's wrong?"

"I'm wet all over! Brr."

"Why?"

"The water's coming in here!"

"Is it?"

"Yes! It's splashing through the port-hole!"

"Um."

At last the port-hole is screwed tight; I have nearly dislocated my fingers, and I am as wet as a herring.

Quick under the blanket again, and tuck the lifebelt under the head—

An agonizing groan.

"What's wrong?"

"*THE BOAT IS ROCKING!*"

"Um."

"I shall be sea-sick!"

"Oh no."

"But the boat is rocking."

"It isn't."

"It's rolling dreadfully!"

"Um."

"You can't feel how much it's rolling?"

"Not at all." True, it does rock, but a woman needn't know everything. And in fact it's rather pleasant; it lifts you up so nicely, then it hesitates for a moment, the boat creaks, and again it undulates downwards; now it's rising under your head—

"Can't you feel it yet?"

"Not in the least." It's queer when suddenly you see your own feet higher than your head; they look rather strange.

"And shan't we sink?"

"Ne-e-ei."

"*Please*, do open that port-hole, or we shall suffocate!"

The husband clambers down from his ironing board, and again opens the port-hole. He might dislocate his fingers with those screws but now it's all the same. "Oh, Lord," he gasps suddenly.

"Do you feel bad too?" inquires a weak and sympathetic voice.

"No, but it is splashing through the port-hole. There is such a lot of water again—"

Silence reigns for a bit except for those heavy sighs. "And is it deep here?" an anxious voice inquires.

"It is. In places up to a mile deep."

"How do you know?"

"I've read it somewhere."

"Jesus Christ! A mile deep!" The sighs grow louder. "How *can* you sleep when it's a mile deep here!"

"Why shouldn't I sleep?"

"But you can't swim!"

"I can."

"But you would be *certain* to drown in such a depth!"

"I should also drown in twenty feet."

"But not so soon." I could hear a low murmuring as if someone was praying. "And can't we get out anywhere?"

"Ne-e-ei."

"Can't you *feel* how much the boat shakes?"

"Jaa."

"It's a *dreadful* storm, isn't it?"

"Um."

Then the *Håkon* makes a fine upward swing and creaks heavily. Cabin bells jingle in the corridor; aha, somebody has been taken ill. It is hardly five o'clock

in the morning and this open sea, they call it *Folda*, is in front of us almost all the way to Rørvik. A nice present. The sighs from the neighbouring berth grow more frequent, they have already almost turned to groans. And then a sudden pause.

The solicitous husband hastens to see what has happened. Nothing. She sleeps like a log.

This kind of tossing on a small boat actually sends one to sleep. Like a cradle.

* * * * *

A sparkling morning, and still the open sea; the rocking is already not so great, but still somehow—well you prefer to stay away from breakfast; you feel better with fresh air. On the deck the captain stands with his feet apart, and beams contentedly.

"The sea was a bit rough last night towards morning, captain, wasn't it?"

"Ne-e-ei. Quite smooth."

* * * * *

But now the islands are here again; these I think are the islands of Dunn's fishermen; brave, smooth rocks just slightly powdered with green. There are dreadful solitudes here; muscular, rounded little islands, and a single little house on them; only a boat, and the sea, and nothing more; not even a tree, not even a neighbour, nothing; only a rock, man and fish. Here man need not go to war to become a hero; it is enough if he feeds himself.

Rørvik, the chief town on the islands; about twenty wooden houses, of which three are hotels, ten cafés, and the editorial office of the local paper; there are about twenty trees, and immense numbers of magpies. We delivered flour there and established loyal friendship with a dog belonging to the place; if you happen to be going that way, it is a cocker-spaniel and most likely it belongs to the local wireless station.

Round the town there is already such a waste land; only stones, dwarf willows, and heather; but it is not really heather but *Empetrum nigrum*, or crow-berry, and it has black and insipidly tart berries some-think like our whortle-berries. A bullock without horns is at pasture there, and he bellows desperately, rather like a boat that is ready to sail; I don't wonder. What isn't rock is almost bottomless peat; every-where it is dug and dried in big heaps; so these are the black pyramids which I saw on the islands while I guessed in vain what they might be. From that peat at any moment they may dig out com-plete ancient trunks and black stumps; in former times there were forests everywhere here, but that must have been many thousands of years ago; good Lord, time flies!

The *Håkon Adalstein* bellowed like the tethered bullock; well, well, we're coming. And if you sailed without us and left us here, I should get used to it too; I should write articles for the local Avisen, and go for walks into a forest of a thousand years ago. What should I write about? Well, actualities, chiefly about infinity, of the last millennium, and what is new among the trolls; and that the nations are arming some-where, and shooting at each other, they say, but that might not be true; don't we, we people from Rørvik, and from the whole district of Vikna, know that man

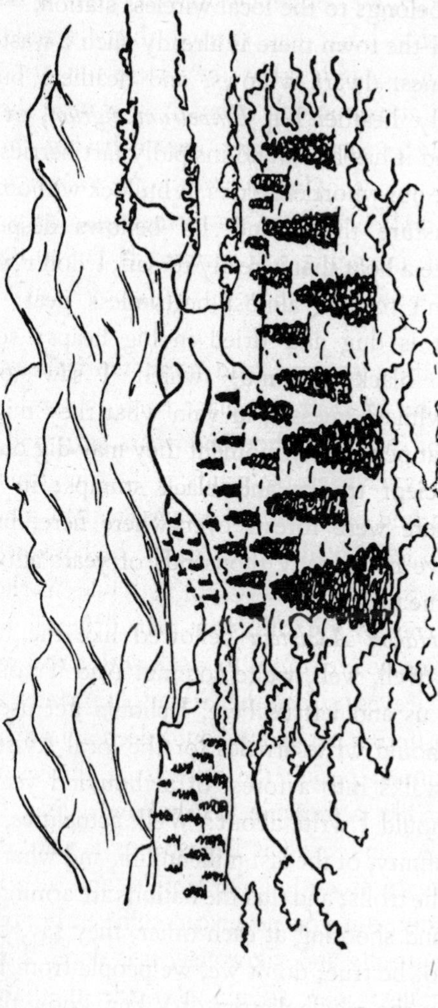

respects man, and is glad to have a good neighbour. And the *Håkon Adalstein* arrived, quite a new and comfortable boat; she carried thirty foreigners of various nationalities, but they were not armed, and were not at war among themselves, instead they were peacefully buying postcards, and behaving altogether like educated people. At twelve the *Håkon* weighed anchor, and set out on its further tour of polar exploration, intending to penetrate as far as Bodø, or even the Lofoten. We wish the happy boat a happy journey!

Well then, onward, and mind the icebergs; they used to be all over the place here, that was only a couple of hundred thousand years ago; and everywhere they have left the prints of their mighty fingers. You can find out here, by watching, their method of work: an iceberg like that files the highest mountains into sharp spikes and steeples, while it slices the smaller ones off smooth, or it planes them into sharp crests. And where it gets to work with a real massif, it pulls its sleeves up, and then it crushes, grinds, scrapes, and files, until it has ground out a deep hollow between the mountain peaks; the sawdust it throws up and rolls out like a moraine, the hollow it makes into a small lake, and from it it suspends a waterfall, and that's all. In fact it's quite simple, and all the same throughout, but you never can sufficiently appreciate how beautifully and vigorously it is done. That's the whole thing: man should also file the large and

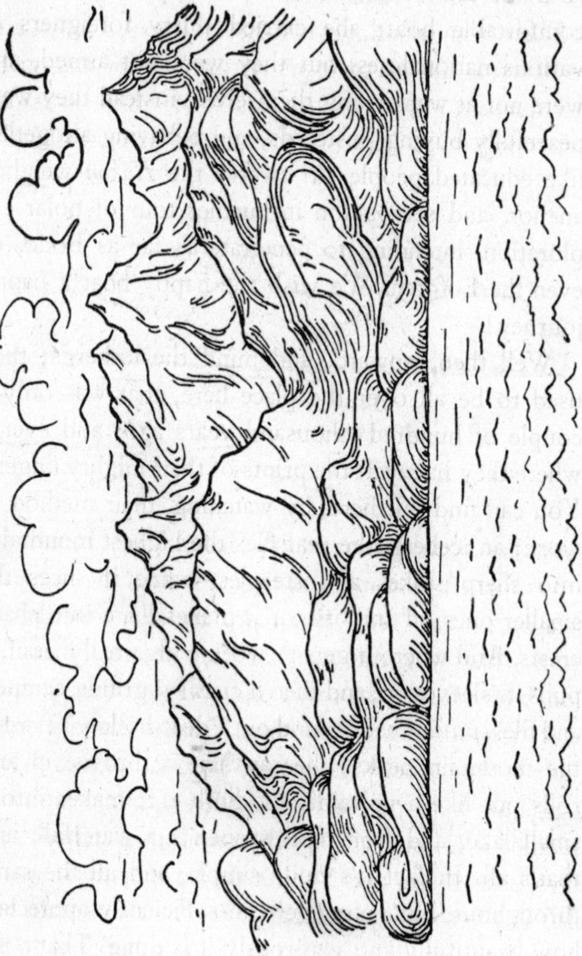

greatest things into height and steepness, and round the small things kindly off.

There is an island, for instance, it is called Leka, and on it is a turned-to-stone virgin whom the giant Hestmannen pursued with his love; there must be something in it, because even to the present day the

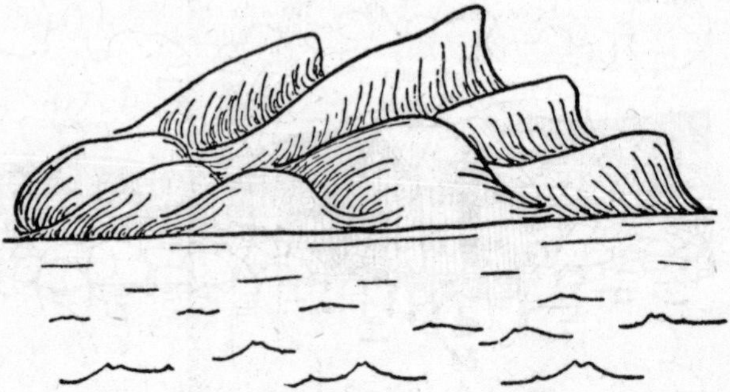

giant has been preserved on Hestmannøy island; he too is turned to stone, and together with the horse he measures 1,845 feet. But there are also other rocks from which you can see that they are really granite floes which forced their way one over the other; it must have been a stirring time then. On the island Torget there is also a rocky mountain, Torghatten, which has a gigantic hole, or corridor, drilled right through the middle; it is long and tall like a Gothic cathedral; I have been there, and I think that originally it was a cleft in the rock into which the top of a mountain has slipped and made a roof; but if there happens to be another legend concerning the origin of Torghatten, suppose that the giants made it, it may also be true, and I give it up. On Torget island there are about a dozen men living; they live chiefly by selling cranberries, lemonade, postcards and sea hedgehogs; one girl, straight and stiff like a wooden statue, was even selling a single red rose; it must have been the greatest

rarity here. Besides that, from that rock corridor there is a marvellous view to both sides of Torghatten: the opal sea and in it the blue islets—

"Won't that rock fall on us?" the anxious soul inquires.

"Ne-e-ei. It will still last a couple of thousand years."

"So *please* do get away from here! Quick!"

* * * * *

And then there is Brønnøy sound and the small town of Brønnøysund inhabited mainly by dried cod. They are dried on long, high fences, and they smell in silence and with Nordic persistence. Altogether up here the world is made of nothing but boulders, cod and sea. We are getting near to the Arctic Circle.

BEYOND THE ARCTIC CIRCLE

That night, I don't know: perhaps I only dreamt

that I got up several times and looked out through that round port-hole in the cabin, and that I could see a landscape on the moon. They were not real mountains, and rocks that projected above the mother-of-pearl sea; they were some kind of strange and dreadful forms; most likely it was only a dream.

Most probably I slept, and in the meantime we crossed the Arctic Circle bellowing gloriously; I heard *Håkon* bellowing but I didn't get up; I thought that it was nothing, that we were only sinking, or calling for help, or something. And in the morning we were already right past the Arctic Circle; it couldn't be helped; we were merely in the Polar regions, without having suitably celebrated this event. All life long we hustle and bustle in the temperate zones like a bird in a cage, and then we are asleep the moment that we cross the line.

If the truth must be told, the first look at the Polar regions is a severe disappointment. These then are the Polar regions? It's not playing fair; for we haven't seen such a green and pleasant land since Molde: little square fields below, human habitations thickly scattered everywhere; above that, mounds and cupolas with billowy leafy growth, and above that—

"Styrman, what is that intensely blue thing over there, hanging from the mountains?"

The good-natured Polar bear from Tromsø who does duty as helmsman with us says: "Ja, that's Svartisen."

Ah, so that's Svartisen; and, after all, what is that Svartisen? It looks nearly like a glacier but it's so incredibly blue; and a glacier perhaps couldn't reach so far down, right among those green groves—

On drawing nearer it really is a birch grove with nothing but brown and white mushrooms, crowberry with black fruit, and creeping juniper, and dryas, spotted orchis, and golden groundsel growing there; and then there is a bare moraine of brown detritus, and then the real glacier reaching down almost to the sea: a huge tongue of glassy ice, sticking out from the firn fields above, between the mountain peaks, about twenty yards thick, nothing but icy boulders, chasms and ledges; and all as blue as smalt, like sulphate of copper, or ultramarine; and if you want to know the reason why it's called the Black Ice, it is because it is so blue that your eyes smart; lower down there is an azure lake between the turquoise ice floes—

"Don't go so near," cries an anxious conjugal voice, "in case it falls down on you!"

The sun grows warmer, fissures rumble in the glacier; right at the foot of the blue ice a pink campion is flowering sweetly. I tell you the world is terribly disconcerting; one day when I shall recall everything that I have seen, I shan't believe that it was true. Only we are lucky to have seen it now; they say that the glacier is always getting smaller, perhaps in twenty thousand years it will be gone, said the styrman; but let us hope that another Ice Age will arrive before then. Up above, that glacier, they say, covers two hundred square miles; well then, I must touch it with my finger—two hundred square miles, that now is something worth while.

Only from a distance can you see how vast it is: the towering mountains, and behind them that white

Svartisen

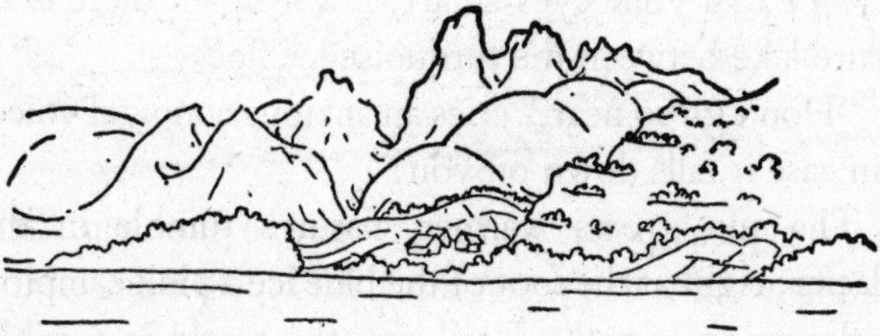

and blue expanse, that is Svartisen; and that crest there, that also is Svartisen, and that one there, that gleams so brightly, that is still more of Svartisen. You come to green islands, Grønøy they are called; grass up to your waist, a luscious and lovely park of willows, alders and aspens, weasels are basking on the boulders;

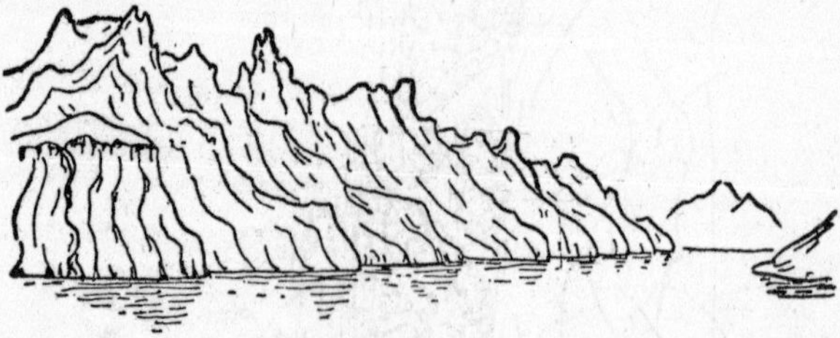

just a typical polar landscape. Above the dear little islands, woolly like green rams, the bluish ridge of the mountains, and behind that a gleaming metallic band: that is Svartisen all the time.

* * * * *

How long ago it is since a little scholar learned: Northern Europe is washed by the warm waters of the Gulf Stream, which has its source in the Gulf of Mexico. He pictured it then as a powerful current bearing to the Polar shores parrots' feathers, coconuts, and God knows what besides. Admittedly there are no coconuts, but otherwise there must be something in it, and now I believe that Northern Europe is washed by the warm Gulf Stream, or some other

Grønøy

form of central heating. Here in Helgeland it must have found it particularly pleasant: it streams slowly

Glomfjord

between the green shores, and breathes warmly almost with emotion. In other places, like Glomfjord, where

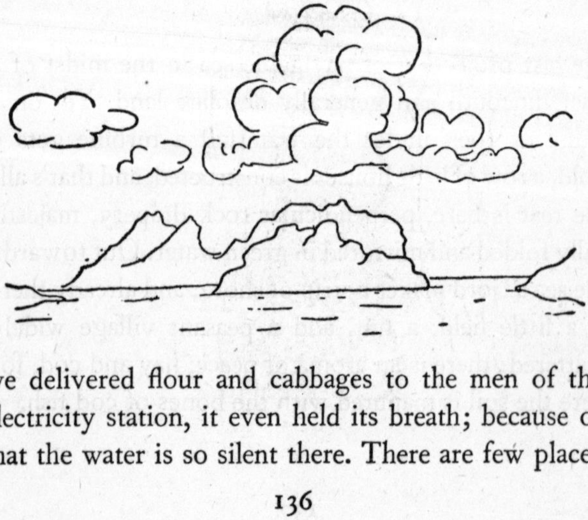

we delivered flour and cabbages to the men of the electricity station, it even held its breath; because of that the water is so silent there. There are few places in the world so strange and still as the furthest end of the deep pocket which is called a fjord. Usually it is quite narrow, and shut in between perpendicular rocks; it is equally the end of the world as well as the last projection of the land into the limitless sea; it is

Glomfjord

the last projection of navigable sea in the midst of a vast, uncouth and generally desolate land. Yet on a ledge of rock under the waterfall a turbine gets a hold, a row of little houses is constructed, and that's all; the rest is bare, perpendicular rock drapery, majestically folded and mirrored in green water. Out towards the sea a fjord makes a strip of shore; and already there is a little field, a hut, and a peasant village widely scattered; there is an aroma of peace, hay and cod, for here the soil is manured with the bones of cod fish.

* * * * *

Thank God, no congregation or collective expedition is travelling with the *Håkon Adalstein*; in fact it is a homely boat. Elsewhere in the world let things be as they may, here we all remained a handful of proud individuals, without leader or shepherd; you could also see it on our faces; with us men life is only tolerable if we are individuals. Here there is a Norwegian doctor with his wife, beautiful and quiet people; and another Norwegian with strong eyebrows like a squirrel's tail; and a young German publisher reminding one of Ferdinand Peroutka, and his young Swiss wife; and a German professor of music, fat, curly-haired and altogether droll; and still another Norwegian doctor, one and all sensible and well versed in the world, who had provided themselves well for the journey at the *vinmonopolet* in Trondheim. Then another pair of Germans, spasmodic and scraggy fellows with glasses; the gentleman keeps scurrying over the deck and taking snapsnots right and left with the rapidity of a machine-gun, while his wife runs after him and verifies with the aid of the map and a guide the name of the mountain; poor thing, she is now one and a half degrees of latitude behind; when we get to Nordkapp, she will have got on the map only as far as Gibostad, and most probably there will be a family row about this. And then two old fragile ladies; I don't know what they are after at Nordkapp, but in these days old ladies are simply everywhere; one day when Colonel Etherton, or some other person,

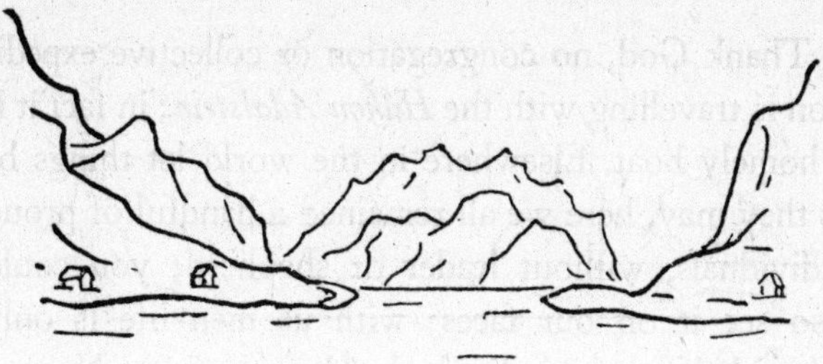

Meløysund

Rosa

climbs to the top of Everest he will be certain to find two or three old ladies there. And still another Norwegian doctor, but he is going home, as far as Hammerfest; he is a young widower with a baby, and he is taking north a bride, a girl like a peach; the round is difficult up there, the young doctor visits the sick right up to Finmarken with a team of reindeer, or across the bays in his motor-boat; he says that it is not very pleasant when he runs short of petrol in a storm during the polar night. And then the so-called engineer, a gentleman of advanced age, who for many years used to act as engineer on boats going to Nordkapp; but now he is somewhere on the land in an electricity station, and he is going on leave to have a look at that Nordkapp; but he hasn't been awake yet since Trondheim, and the professor of music who shares the cabin with him says that he is a most awful drinker. Neat alcohol, he says, and stuff like that. And still there are five Norwegian teachers, or post-office clerks; they appear collectively, it is true, but since they do not form a majority on the boat they are completely harmless. And a swarm of Norwegian scouts, long-legged rascals who camp in the bows; but there are fewer of them than there were yesterday, they must have fallen overboard on the way; on the Lofoten we shed them all.

* * * * *

At Meløysund the engineer in the wicker chair on the deck awakes and falls hopelessly for the young Swiss lady; he gazes at her with heavy, misty eyes, and shows visible signs of sobriety.

Meantime the mountains file past in all their beauty; here gleaming like crowns, there clouded and glowering; one has a solitary and terribly clear individuality, while the others shake hands with each other and are content to form a massif. Each has a different face and thinks by himself; I tell you, Nature is a tremendous individualist, and to everything she creates she gives character; but we human beings haven't enough understanding for that. Only it is good that we give each mountain a proper name, as we do to human beings;

objects simply exist, while personalities have also their names; this mountain is called Rota, that one Sandhorn, and so on. Mountains, ships, dogs, and bays have their proper names: that alone marks them as individualities.

Bodø (Landegode)

There is a rock there, it is called Landegode, and it is just behind the town of Bodø; and it is so symmetrical that it looks like an artificial decoration, but it may be real; all the same, men come to point it out to one another, and they assert that behind it you can make out the outline of the Lofoten. Poor Landegode was so beautifully blue against the golden sky, and the golden mother-of-pearl of the sea, that it seemed undignified. A downright mountain ought not to be so handsome; it's, well, unmanly somehow.

"Ja," said the styrman, "it was just here that a boat sank last year."

LOFOTEN

Let us not grudge things their due: we do not speak of Lofots, but of Lofoten, although it is a whole group of islands, not counting the islets, rocks, sand-banks and single boulders which lie scattered here in the sea with no meagre generosity; you know, when in Norway you count a hundred and fifty thousand islands and islets, they are bound to strike the eye somewhere.

The first morning glance through the cabin port-hole at Lofoten reveals to the amazed eye, first of all, a strange multitude of boulders in the most varied configurations; they are completely bald, and golden brown on the milky opal sheet of water, and only in places, from their armpits, tufts of wiry grass are sprouting; pleasant round boulders worn smooth by the breakers, rock towers carved out by the storms, collections of stones, groups of ledges, or solitary stones; here and there a small lighthouse, or single tower, here and there an erection of very long poles, perhaps for drying cod; this then is Lofoten. And then one goes up on deck to see still more of it, and one perceives that up from this embroidery of boulders a bouquet of mountains sprouts up to heaven.

A bouquet of mountains: you can't express it in any other way; and here you can see that the world blossomed in granite before it could flower in bird-cherry and lilac. "And God said: Let the waters under the heaven be gathered together unto one place, and

Lofoten

let the dry land appear: and it was so. And God called the dry land Earth; and the gathering together of the waters called He the Sea: and God saw that it was good." It was in fact very good, nay, just superb; in Lofoten, however, the dry land arose not in one place, but in a considerable number of places which God

called Moskenesøy, Flakstadøy, Vestvegøy, and many other names, and He endowed them with a special power; and in those dry places boulders and rocks began to flourish as nowhere else in the world; and then mountains began to spring up like trees in a wood; there is granite enough so that they could grow as if of the water—in fact, they really do grow straight up from the water: some bushy like ashes, oaks, and elms, and other high and steep like spruces, birches, or poplars; and a garden of mountains was brought forth which is called Lofoten; and it was good. You say, bare rock; but it gives you more the impression of something brimming over, of terrible abundance and exuberance; vain glory, every thoroughgoing creation works with a surplus, and without substantial phantasy even mountains cannot appear. Therefore you have to go as far as Lofoten to see what can be done with each material, even if it is material as heavy as granite, gneiss, biotite gneiss, and primordial schist.

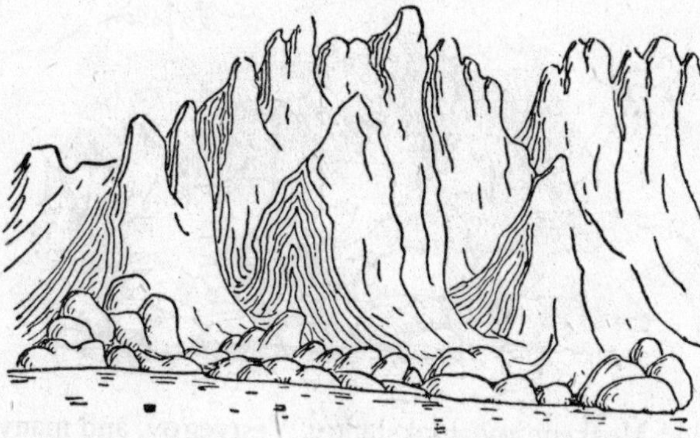

As for the people, most probably they can't live from the rocks, and therefore they live from the gathering together of the waters which God called the seas; and they catch flounders, salmon, sea trout and chiefly cod. No matter whether such a place is called Balstad, Leknes, Stamsund, Henningsvær, or Kabelvåg, everywhere there is a wooden harbour on piles, where to the eager rumbling of the crane we unload the fruits of the South, like cabbages, flour, cement, and red bricks; and in return we take on board cases with cod, barrels with cod, boxes with cod, or hundreds of bundles of dried cod; they are tied together merely with string like brushwood, and they look like bundles of some dry, twisted, and cracking bark; only a penetrating smell indicates that it is something to eat. Besides that, there are a dozen wooden houses, of which nine are little coffee-houses

called *kafistova*, one the post-office, two shops with an assortment of tins, sweets and tobacco, and one the publishing office of the local Avisen. All the rest (apart from the telegraph poles and rocks) is nothing but cod hanging on long poles and racks, smelling of rancid glue, and rustling softly in the Nordic breeze. I should have liked to learn something more about the life of the fishermen in Lofoten, but at this time of the year perhaps they only dry the cod that they caught in the Spring; I tell you, it is a hard and heroic life.

There are places, for instance, like Melbo (but that already is in Vesterålen), where the frames for drying

Henningsvaer

the cod are the highest erections in the town; they are complete cod cathedrals, where instead of the organ there is the rumbling of milliards of flies, and the smell of the cod rises to heaven like the incense of the North; and all around them hundreds of thousands of severed and desiccated cod skulls grin at you with provocation. There is (that is, in Melbo) a bridge across the green sea bay; that bay at the same time is the local rubbish tip, and the sojourner for a long time may spit into the water, and observe on the bottom of the bay old tins, dead cats, sea stars, seaweed, broken bits of pot, hoops, and putrefaction, all turquoise and silvery, dematerialized and magically phosphorescent in the pool of limpid green. As well as that a sea devil twisted and turned lazily in the ooze, while upright and solitary a bottle of beer, still unopened, stood on the sea bottom; perhaps some diver or triton set it up there.

Or while the boat is discharging the flour for Lofoten the traveller may step out on shore, and go perhaps on foot from Kabelvåg to Svolvær; and then behind a rocky, bare promontory towards the sea, an alpine green country appears with pastures, and abundance of aspens and alders; and round every little wooden house a small garden where gloriously, and almost frantically, monskhood and larkspur are in flower, and in every tiny window scarlet geraniums and dark crimson begonias with large flowers—what a feast of flowers beyond the Arctic Circle! And he will find a quiet bay, where he will bathe, and

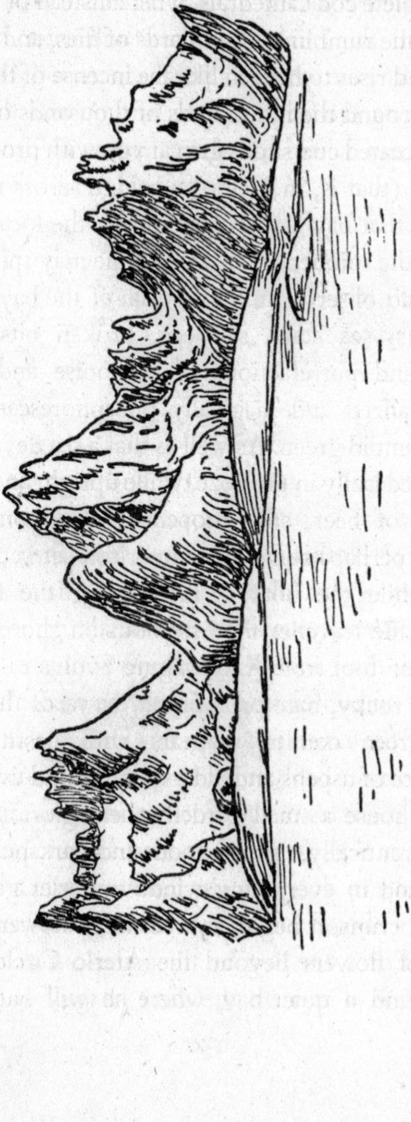

bask in the sixty-eighth degree of latitude, and then, looking very blue, he will assert that it was a divine swim; and the local inhabitants will offer him their huts where the pilgrim with chattering teeth will dress among the fishing nets. And he will discover a green-house where climbing roses are in flower,

and tomatoes are getting ripe, and then he will sail onwards from Svolvær, perhaps to Brettesnes. And what there? Nothing, we deliver flour there; and the inhabitants of that place will come to have a look at us, the local beauties will promenade along the harbour, and two or three more enterprising young fellows will board our ship in order to inspect the whole boat with the eye of the expert; they do this kind of thing everywhere, most probably it is one of the customary diversions and pastimes of the North. Almost everywhere a grey shaggy dog awaits us at the harbour, he slips on board, and lies down at our feet; and when the boat has already hooted for the third time, the styrman must come, and drag the dog by the collar out of the boat. It appears as if it were the same shaggy one all the time; before we reach every harbour, we are already looking forward to seeing if 'our dog" will welcome us there by wagging his bushy tail.

Well, good-bye, doggy, we are journeying on again; and this then is Raftsundet, this smooth and bright

channel between the mountain peaks; this path between two lines of glaciers, towers and precipices, this way between the bastions of moraines and débris of avalanches, a pilgrimage along an avenue of mountains; this way one ought to sail to the king's castle in Ultima Thule, but this is only the way one sails to Melbo. It is all the same wherever we happen to be going; every harbour is merely a little station of reality along a journey that is a dream; but when you sail through Raftsund you ought to come to nowhere, and dissolve together with the boat into a mere mirage. And then the people in Melbo and in Stokmarknes would enquire why the *Håkon Adalstein* has not arrived to-day? Well, it hasn't; maybe it has dissolved through sheer enchantment in Raftsund, and it has become a phantom of a boat; that happens sometimes at Ultima Thule.

Everywhere on the earth there are hours around midday when the whole world seems flat. sober, and rather uninteresting, most probably because the sun stands high in the sky and throws only short shadows; these never make objects plastic enough. Here in the North it is different; here the sun is always so low down near the horizon that objects cast shadows in a long and rich manner as they do with us towards the end of the day; as they do with us when the magic hours of the late afternoon are reached, when the light turns golden, and the shadows lengthen, and objects recede further away, stand out in finer outline, and with more relief than in the white and perpendicular heat of the day; and you see, extremely sharply, every dear feature on the face of the earth, but with the seducing and sublime detachment of distance. The northern day has the finesse of the fifth hour; and if I might choose, well then, I say, give me the northern light.

And suddenly the *Håkon Adalstein* turns and sails straight towards the barrier of rocks; only at the last moment a narrow gap takes form, and the boat sails in between perpendicular walls upon silent and immovable water like the surface of a mirror; this is the goblin's bay, or Trollfjord, and it does look like it.

Quoting from an expert source, Trollfjord is "*en viden kjent fjord, trang med veldige tinder på begge sider*";

begge sider most likely means both sides, and *veldige tinder* is perhaps something like walls of rock; in actual fact there are rock walls on either side, but that is not what is strange: more terrible is it that you lose the certainty of what is above and what is beneath—such a dumb and bottomless mirage it is there. The boat also glides softly and eerily as if she were afraid of it all; she floats upon a narrow strip of sky between steep walls, which like precipices sink up and down; and right above the blue fjord of heaven opens out. I don't know, but perhaps it looks something like this in the other world: there also, most likely, objects swim in infinite unreality, and man must feel terribly creepy there.

* * * * *

So you needn't grumble that I shall throw in for you with Lofoten the whole of Vesterålen as a makeweight; this also is an archipelago, but it didn't quite manage to make itself independent; for instance, one part of the island of Hinnøy is reckoned with Lofoten, and the other half with Vesterålen, and it is just the same with Austvågøy. If I were in their place I should decide for Lofoten, but I decline to get myself mixed up in their personal affairs.

Vesterålen is a place prolific with dried cod and clouds; when we arrived there young clouds were just being hatched out. At such times a wisp of fog begins to rise from a rock crater, it climbs speedily higher and gets caught on the top of the mountain; there for a time it flutters like a flag, it shakes itself out, unfolds; after that it detaches itself, starts on its journey, and

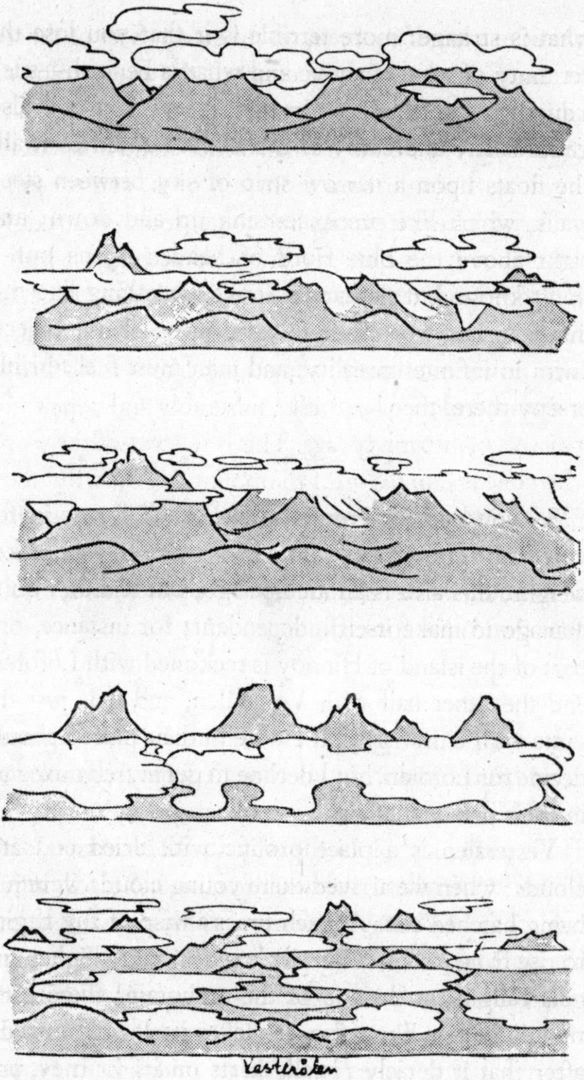

Vesterålen

sprinkles a handful of rain on the steely sheet of the sea. At times like that in our country the meteorological stations report that a depression is approaching. And again at another time a small white cloud floats in the sky, it gets caught on a mountain peak, and it cannot get any further; it would like to get loose, it struggles but maybe it develops a tear, or something; it begins to droop and deflate, and slowly it sinks, it settles down on the mountains like a heavy featherbed, it rains down over them, something like a thick broth, or cream, and then languidly, miserably and hopelessly, it dissolves into misty rags. This is the way of the world when one is unmindful of the mountain peaks. But these misty shreds recover again in the lap of the mountains; they begin to ascend rapidly, and so on; in Vesterålen, in Iceland, in Greenland, and in other places, this is how clouds are formed.

* * * * *

In Melbo the passenger, said to be the engineer, again began to drink, this time perhaps from sorrow; behind it I think there was that pretty Swiss. He drank pure alcohol all the way to Stokmarknes, after which, somewhere short of Sortland, he fell into a coma; the German professor of music who shared his cabin tucked him up carefully, and the whole night long he was with him watching anxiously whether he was still alive. I say the whole night long, but there was no night; only round about midnight it became rather vague, and strange, the heart felt oppressed, the people quietened down, the cheerful German professor spoke with tears in his eyes of the death of his mother, and then again it was already bright daylight. Well, what is there to do; one goes to sleep, and doesn't know really why. And suddenly, crash!

"Did you hear that bang?"

"Um," mumbles the husband.

"Haven't we struck something?"

"Ne-e-ei."

"Then what was the bang?"

". . . . perhaps a tyre burst, eh?"

But it wasn't a tyre; only a whaling boat a few yards away from us that shot a harpoon at a whale. Just one's luck to miss it.

TROMS

"*Litt bagbord*," commands the small officer on the bridge.

"*Litt bagbord*," repeats the man at the helm, and turns the wheel.

"*Hart bagbord!*"

"*Hart bagbord.*"

"*Stödig!*"

"*Stödig.*"

Here to the left, this is Trondenes Kirke; the oldest little stone church in the district, still fenced in to the present day with ramparts. It is a grey day, a grey sea with white plumes of waves, at times a sprinkle of cold rain. Below in the cabin the engineer is snoring; he hasn't been awake for twenty-four hours, and the fat German professor is nearly worn thin with the strain. True, he can't speak a word of Norwegian, and ever since Trondheim the engineer hasn't been able to

Trondenes Kirke

talk at all, but once men live together, they have, dash it all, a bit of feeling for one another, haven't they?

"*Litt styrbord*," says the officer.

"*Litt styrbord.*"

"*Stödig!*"

"*Stödig*," repeats the man at the helm, and gazes with blue eyes into the milky distance.

The clouds are lifting, it will be a fine day after all. That little wet, grey harbour, that is Rolla; only mist, stones, and cod-fish, and mountains above it, all the time, all the time nothing but mountains and clouds.

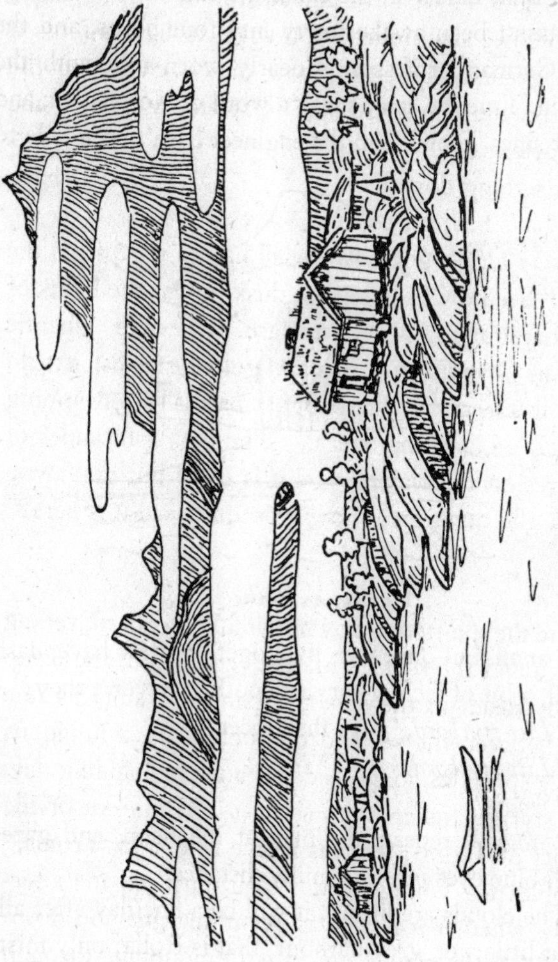

Rolla

But as soon as we have unloaded flour for the people of Rolla we shall journey on again to have a look at more clouds. My Gosh, how one is chilled to the bone on the windward side! Captain, what does the barometer say?

"It's going down."

"That's bad, isn't it?"

"Ne-e-ei, it's good. We shall have a wind from the west." See how in the green dusk, under the lights of the harbour, rainbow medusas rise like gigantic gobbets of sputum; scarlet and golden star-fish extend their fibrous arms; what a lot of small fish are swarming about here, and that eternal, shimmering meander of pictures on the water—yes, it is cold; but don't you see on the other hand how beautifully sad it is here?

* * * * *

And the spluttering downpour falls on board, veiling the sea and the rocks with a silvery tissue; the damp boards steam in the sun, the rainbow vaults its fine arch between the sea and the mountains, a luminous drizzle sprinkles down, and it is a tender, shining day. The styrman takes us to show us the interior of the district of Troms; it is his native land. "Ja, Troms," mumbles the young giant. "You must tell me afterwards, whether it is also as beautiful with you down below." And he drives you into the mountains through a long valley of birches, and of forests, through a valley of roaring torrents, through a valley of wooden huts covered with turf; small lakes in the birch forest, full of blue trout; little brooks sinking under the rocks, fallen avalanches of stone from ancient times overgrown with trees long ago, brown peat soil covered with cranberries, and whortleberries, ferns, marsh-

grass, and strong willows—the styrman is right. A dark lake at the bottom of the dale, over the brown boulders a green and silver river falls in cascades, veils of waterfalls hang on the mountains. The styrman is right.

Behind the brown village circular huts, all of turf: these are the first Laplanders that we have met; they are, in fact, living here, but the misery is dreadful; any amount of children, all rickety, and shy like dormice. The huts have a framework of poles, covered with turf, and they are held up a bit by stones and beams; a tin pipe is stuck on top, and that's all; and at least a dozen people live in it. What do they live on, I can't tell, but they do not beg, nor do they steal; quite a number are fair and blue-eyed, but you can see by their eyes and cheek-bones that it is another world, after all.

The styrman is right: the Northern forest is endless, even if it is only a gnarled and stunted birch, somewhat spectral with its white branches; even if it is only an occasional knotted pine; even if it is only a thicket of dwarf alders and willows; even if it is only the stumps and stubs of something that used to be a forest until man, and avalanche, or some other catastrophe occurred. In fact it's more like a tundra than a forest; there is so little soil that they cannot even set their telegraph poles in the ground, and they must wall them round with stones to make them stand. For miles of the way (I am, of course, reckoning in nautical miles) there is no human habitation, except for a tumbledown Lapland hut; and yet on the edge of the tundra, on a birch tree, a post box is hanging; if I knew who collected the letters from it I would send him greetings at Christmas, and postcards from different towns and countries, so that they would reach that lonely box in the Northern forest. And because here in the mountains they cannot dry fish, at least on wooden stands they dry the peat; I have drawn all this so that everybody may see that the styrman was right, and Troms is the most beautiful region in the world. I have also drawn the hornless Norwegian cattle

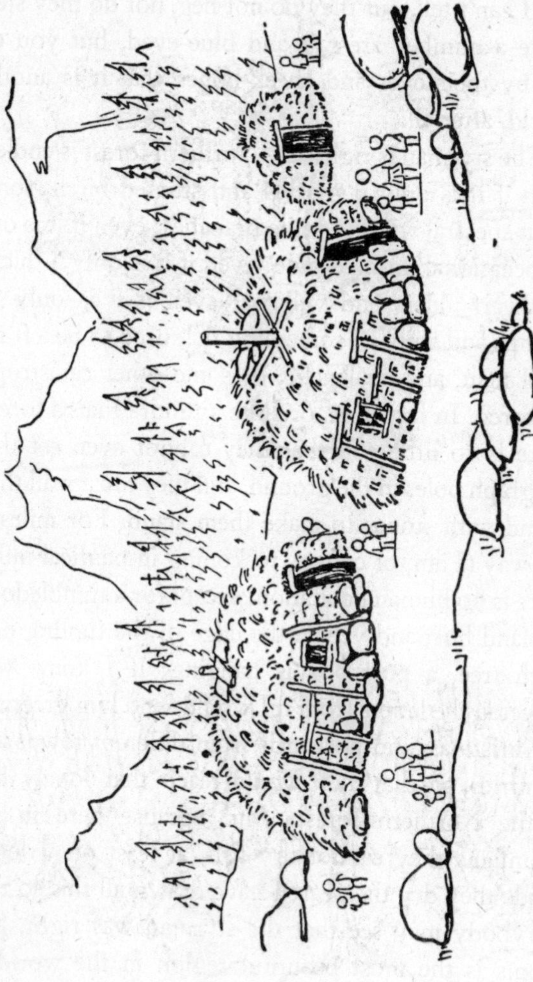

grazing among the birches on the spiky tufts of grass, but I did not know how to draw Bardufos; it is too big, and I don't know how to draw a waterfall that

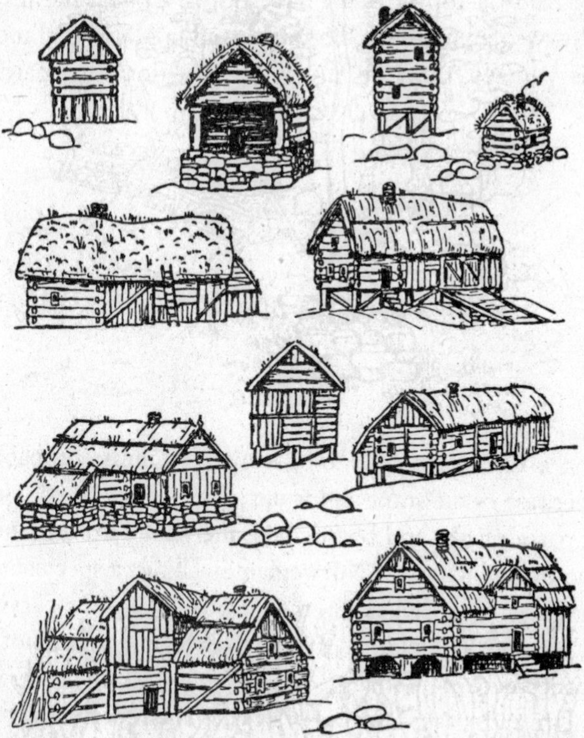

would turn the beholder's head, and give him a dreadful desire to jump into that flying and thundering and foamy water. Instead I have drawn the valley of Målselv, with the lake-like sheet of the river, where a ferry-boat took us across; the snow above was pink, and the mountains richly gilded, and Målselv was blue, green, and gold—I say, the styrman was right; *ja, en herlig tur.*

And on top of that I have drawn as well the little Norwegian houses in Bardudal, and in Målselvdal too; as you see, they are built partly on tiny legs, partly

on a Cyclopian wall to sustain them, most probably because of the snow and water; they are timbered with brown planks and boards laid alternately upright and across, which gives Norwegian dwellings a special and expressive appearance; they have pleasantly carved shutters, the windows full of flowers, and instead of a roof there is a shaggy cap of moss, grass, willow-herb, and sometimes also of birches and firs. Really, the styrman was right.

"Ja," mumbles the young giant. "But wait till you see Tromsø." For in Tromsø the styrman has a wife.*

* Tromsø, said to be the Paris of the North, the capital of the district of Troms; ten thousand inhabitants, the seat of *vinmonopolet*, bishop, and of expeditions for seals; besides that, it is noted

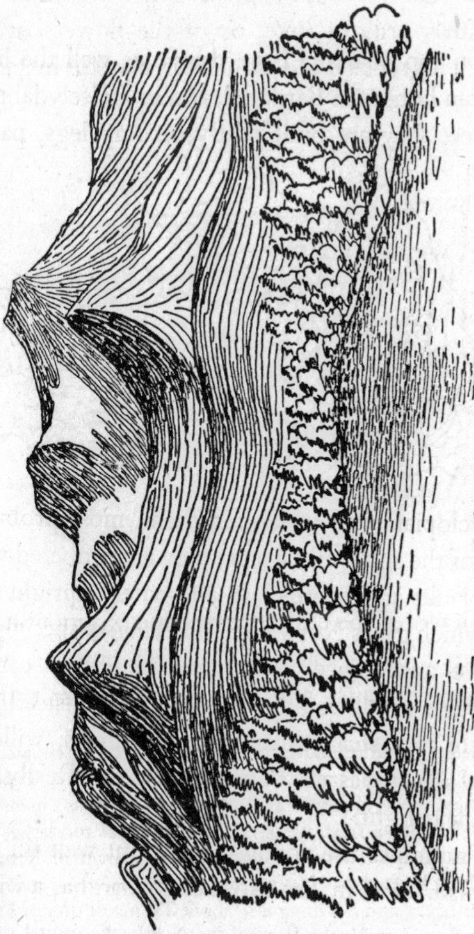

Målselv

SUNDS AND FJORDS

I know that one can't express it in words; one can speak with words of love, or of the flowers of the field, but with rocks it is difficult; can one, for instance,

describe in words the outline and shape of a mountain? I know that one speaks of fantastic outlines, wild peaks, huge massifs, and so on, but it isn't that;

for its museum, beautiful surroundings, and for being situated on Latitude 70. A brisk trade in post-cards, chocolate, Lapland babouches, and tobacco, as well as in Arctic furs; here, as a memento I could have bought a fresh walrus head, but it was too large, and its smell was dreadful. The pavements of the town of Tromsø are profusely enlivened with Lapps in national costumes, and with stuffed polar bears, and anything else about Tromsø I do not know—only that from here Amundsen flew with the French airmen on his last journey North; a little monument close by the harbour refers to it.

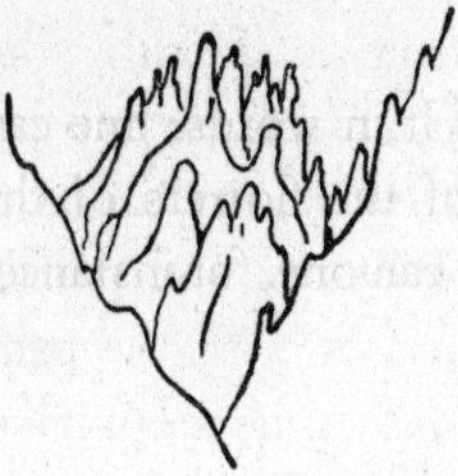

Lyngsfjord

merely with words you can't run as if with your thumb along the crests of the mountains, or nip between thumb and finger the highest points, so as to sense with delight their edges, fractures, and polish; with words it is impossible to feel as with the palm of your open hand the ramifications of the mountains, their bony skeleton, their powerful limbs and sinewy joints, their terrific necks, loins and thighs, shoulders and bodies, knees and legs, joints and muscles; God, what anatomy, what beauty! what superb, bald beasts they are! I tell you, all this can be seen and sensed with the eyes, for the eyes are a divine instrument, and the best part of the brain: they are more sensitive than the tips of the fingers, and sharper than the point of a knife; what a lot can one do with one's eyes, but words, I say, are good for nothing; and I shall not say any more about what I saw.

I say, with numb fingers I tried to draw things which I saw; wind or no wind, I had to sketch one mountain after the other: here that terribly massive one, piled up into athletic shoulders, groins and hips, like an animal at rest; or that fair one, heaped up like sand, as if somebody had piled and thrown it up with a shovel out of nothing but ruins; or that one that looks like Pharaoh's throne, with moraines for arms, and a glacier like the crater of a volcano; that one nibbled like a slice of bread, this spiky one with needles of schist, and what do I know besides; if only I were a geologist to know what caused it all! With a

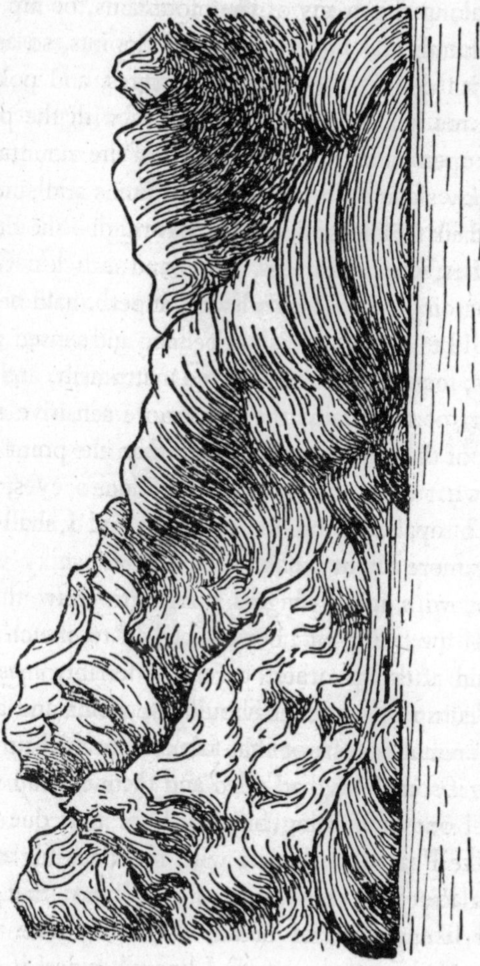

frozen nose I snuffle over my notebook on the windward side, and rub my chilled hands in the lee, so that no mountain may escape me; but what is one to do, all the time it is not the proper thing; air, I say, and colour, cannot be drawn, they must be depicted in words, or something; such shadows there are, transparent like chalcedony, smooth like metal, outstretched like a fabric; such golden and oblique light, such a nacreous, clear and satin sea, such blue and bell-clear air; and there, where the sea touches the earth, there is a thin silvery line, glistening like mercury; but as for the sea, it is impossible to do anything more with it either in pencil or in words.

Yes, the vast ocean alone is simply inexpressible; it has its moments of fearful indigo blue, or of steely grey or of opal, flowing brightness; it is touched with the snow-white crests of the spring tide, spiky with short, sharp ripples, or with long stripes from the rollers of the heavy sea; but all that, I say, is nothing compared with the water of the Norwegian *sunds*. Here it is in ripples, and silvery like a mountain lake; you sail round the bar of the island, the water turns leaden grey, and long rollers with white crests begin to hand on to each other the boat. That wave there on the horizon, it will be a fine one; it rolls straight on towards the ship, now it gathers all its strength, rumbles, thunders, and dashes towards us; but its reckoning was wrong, we cut through it and hardly shook at all; but another is already upon us, it sinks

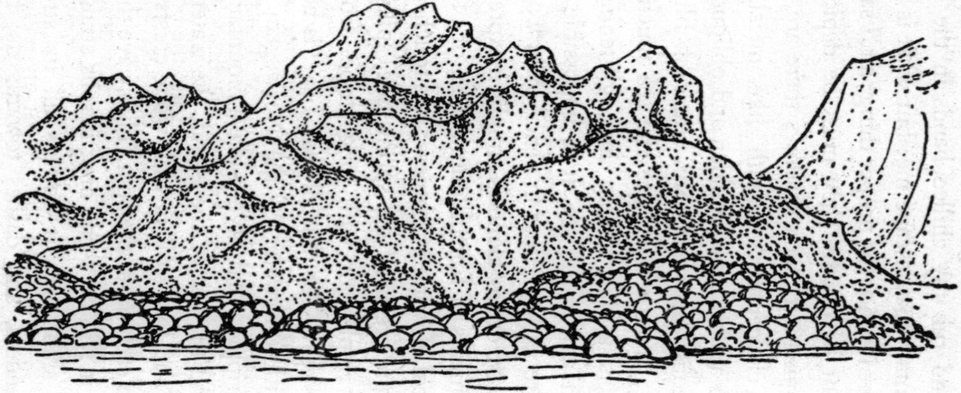

Tromsøysfjord

beneath the boat, and now it lifts us up upon its shoulders; can't you feel how it bears us up? Ha, that was one! So, and now we sink while the stern is coming up; how far will it climb? It stops, and waits for a moment; then there is a cracking and a fizzling, and all the time the *Håkon* softly sways from side to side, and

from bow to stern, and the water splashes right on board; and the traveller clings to the rails, and he feels like shouting for joy; that's the real thing, old chap! Look out, look out, there is a still finer one coming; its claws are white, and it hunches up as if to pounce; and suddenly it dissolves beneath the boat. Oh no, it doesn't, it has already got hold of us; the bow slips steeply down, and what will come next? Nothing; the whole boat glides gently and smoothly down, and creaks with delight in all its joints. And now, let us say, we are again on the lee side of an island; only choppy waves strike the side of the boat with unpleasant thuds; across the *sund* there is the glitter of a silvery line; quite unprepared we sail along a long lake that is tenderly and sweetly rippled; through its thousands of tiny, scintillating facets, blue and golden rocks, with white snows above, make their image. The *sund* narrows, it is already only just a little path between the rocks; here the water subsides into absolute

unreality, deeply green, as smooth as oil, and silent like a dream; you must not even breathe so as not to disturb and shatter in it that terrible and unblemished picture of the mountains; only behind the boat, in the undulating water from the keel, is the trail of a superb peacock's tail. The mountains move apart, and a vast bright sheet is filled with the sky, crinkled like silk the better to shine, glistening and nacreous, and soft like oil; in lithesome, gliding flashes the gold and amethyst chains of the mountains are mirrored in it! God, what am I to do with it! But that is still not the right thing; a sund is only a sund; on the other hand a fjord is, how shall I say it; in short, it is no longer of this world, and it is impossible to draw it, describe it, or play it on a violin; dear me, I give it up; as if I could report on something that is not of this world! Briefly, it is all rock, and below is the smooth water in which everything is reflected; and that's it. And on those rocks

eternal snow is lying, and waterfalls hang down like veils; that water is transparent, and green like emerald, or something, and as quiet as death, or like infinity, and terrible like the Milky Way; and these mountains are quite unreal, because they do not stand upon any shore, but on a mere bottomless mirage; haven't I told you that it is all an illusion! And sometimes, when in the genuine world the evening hour draws near, such a fine and straight veil of mist rises from that water, and above it peaks and chains of mountains raise themselves, of cosmic nebulous breath; and so you see, didn't I tell you that it is another world? And this is not the *Håkon Adalstein*, but a phantom boat which glides without sound on the silent expanse; and it is the zero hour, which on the human planet they call midnight, but in this world there is no night, or time. And I saw midnight rainbows hanging from one shore to the other; a mild and golden sunset mirrored

Lyngsfjord

in the sea before a frosty morning dawn; I saw evening and morning glows dissolve in the tremulous radiance of the waters, the silver comb of the sun teased the sparkling sheet of the ocean; then the shiny paths of the tritons began to sparkle fearsomely on the sea, and it was day. Goodnight, goodnight, for it is already day, the first hour; the mountains have screened themselves with a luminous veil, to the North the open sund is glistening white, the sea gurgles coldly, and the last shivering passenger on board begins to read another book.

HARBOURS AND LANDING PLACES

Sure enough, I should almost have forgotten the harbours; but here there are no more any longer,

Lyngseidet

except for Lyngseidet, and Skjervøy, and that place, what's its name, where so many wild larkspurs, willow-herbs, alpine lettuce, and dead nettles flourished; it doesn't matter now, but in Lyngseidet is a small white church of wood among the fishing nets set out to dry, and heaps of small, two-wheeled carriages for the tourists, and a little further along, in a green valley, there is a settlement of real Lapp nomads; these, in fact, arrive with the beginning of the tourist season,

and they live here in their original semi-wild manner, milking the reindeer, performing magic, and selling to the tourist jack-knives carved from reindeer antlers, Lapp babouches, embroideries, and Arctic dogs. To the best of my knowledge the Lapps make a living chiefly by running about Narvik, Tromsø, or Hammerfest in picturesque costumes (with tight trousers, beaklike slippers, belted coats, and red plumes in their caps) and to the foreigners they sell wooden spoons, furs, and reindeer antlers; and then by living in tents

and letting themselves be photographed. In other respects they are very modest, of slight build, and degenerate; and they have an amazing, truly savage ear.

"Čapku," I was addressed in Czech, "come and look at this kid!"

"Čapku, come and look at this kid!" repeated a grinning Lappish woman distinctly and faultlessly.

"Čapku," mumbled a shrivelled old fellow, "come and look at this kid! Čapku! Čapku!"

"Čapku," clamoured the whole camp.

"Karle, do you hear what they say?" said someone to me in Czech.

"Karle, do you hear what they say?" the camp repeated exuberantly.

"Čapku, come and look at this kid!"

"Čapku! Čapku!"

"They are rascals," I exclaimed aloud.

The old Lapp woman nodded her head gravely. "They are rascals," she said, "Karle, do you hear what they say? Čapku, come and look at this kid!"

(Well, then I sketched that kid. Unfortunately he was not for sale.)

* * * * *

Yes, but coming back to those harbours: they are all alike, and they only differ in size. In some places it is only a wooden shed, and nothing else besides, except for one or two fishermen's huts, brown and dusky like the rocks on which they stand; in some other places around the harbour, and its paunchy warehouses, a complete little town spreads out, one *hotelet*,

nine *kafistov*, two or three *forretningen* with all possible kind of goods, a newspaper office, and sometimes also a church. By day there is nothing to it, it is dull, clean, and rather forsaken; but when the anchors are dropped (I mean to say, when the boat is tied up in the harbour) at the zero hour, or at one, two o'clock in the morning, it has its strange and wistful charm; everything is closed, but the children play by the harbour, young men and girls promenade along the main street, and a group of the local gentry shuffles up on to the brygge to have chin-wag with the captain, or the styrman, on the way the world is going, and other news; most probably in that bright night, in that unreal midnight light they have no desire at all for sleep. And then it dawns upon one that in winter, on

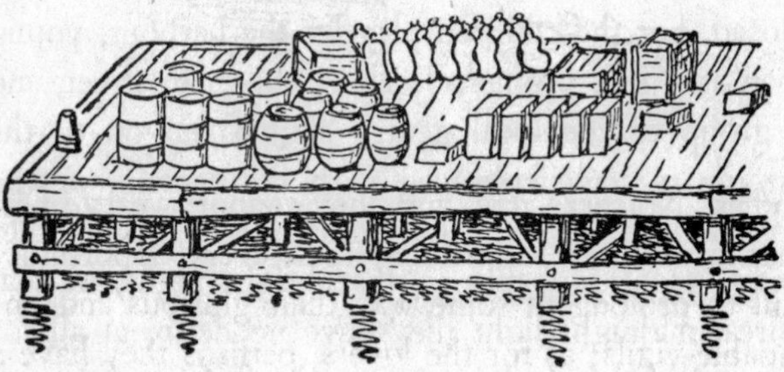

that handful of clean little houses, for weeks and months lies a Polar night; now they are enjoying their

endless Northern day, and they cannot weary of it; that is why like loafers they seize every opportunity still to prolong in some way their glorious and unsatiable vigils; as for the lovers, perhaps they have a

rendezvous behind the nearest cloud, for there are no groves, or dusks. And the traveller gazes with a deeper understanding upon the respectable little town which for nothing on earth would go to bed, and a thought warms his heart a little that here he is helping to deliver cabbage, salted beef, and agreeable excitement.

And while we are talking about harbours we must not forget the lighthouses, floating buoys, and various kinds of all types of navigation signals which line our way almost like an avenue. Now in that clear night they do not even blink with red and white lights; but God bless you for shining for ships and men during the winter's night. God bless you, solitary turret, hello fishing hut, how do you do, cruising steamer that overtakes us on the way to Nordkapp; we shall not race with you, because we are carrying a cargo for men; but greet we may because on the sea it is the custom. Just to let you know, this last night we dropped anchor in the open sund because someone rowing in a boat waved to us; and we took on board a lady who had nothing with her but a geranium in a pot; that's the ship we are, sir. No bright and luxurious steamer, but a small boat with men, and cabbages, and

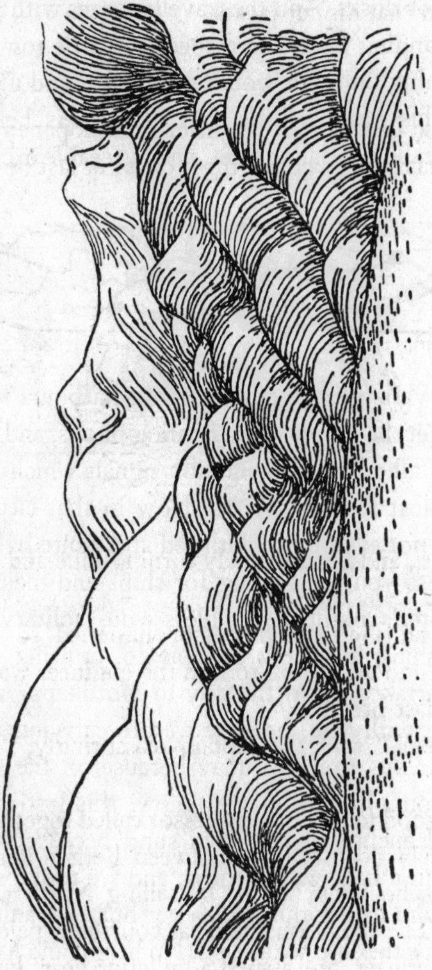

flour, and my compliments, mind that you don't catch a chill in that dinner jacket.

* * * * *

In case I forget, the engineer hasn't opened his eyes yet; it has continued for three days; at last he gave up

wheezing, and began slowly turning blue and shaking his chin.

The fat German professor hastened to tell the captain; and according to him the engineer was drawing his last breath.

"Ne-e-ei," said the captain reassuringly, "I know him."

The good fellow of a professor called together three Norwegian doctors from between Bergen and Hammerfest who happened to be sailing North with the *Håkon.* The illustrious medical concilium paid a visit to the engineer, and issued a bulletin: heart bad, liver ruined, kidneys perished; the fellow will last another couple of years. There were great rejoicings over that, and much whisky, gin, and aquavit was spilt on it; but nothing happened to anybody, and in the morning the engineer was already up on board, sober and terribly embarrassed; and he enjoyed the general sympathies.

* * * * *

Yes, there was still one more bay, it was called Altafjord, or Altenfjord; it was very beautiful, and very pearly; besides other things, I noticed there how the hills are born: simply by sprouting, you know. A mountain like that which is farrowing, calving, puts out a long arm, this becomes constricted in several places, and forms from itself small hillocks; filamentous and unicellular algae do so in the same way.

And from there they took us up along the Altaelv on to the mountain plateau in Finmarken; they drove us through a green valley of pleasant, squat farms, through a deep pool of woods, past the sides of the waterfalls, beside peaty lakes and tiny pools; and then only dwarf birch, and stones, and creeping willow; still a bit higher up, and there already is the roof of Norway; a bare plain without end, a huge granite floe slightly undulating, and slightly fissured, nothing but erratic blocks, or small rocky terraces, nothing but tiny swamps, all quagmire; except that every few yards there is a pile of stones with a cross, that's for the people to know which way to go when the snow falls. And it is all deadly, ghastly, pallid; that is the white lichen's doing; delicate like lace, and pale like mildew; besides that the cotton-grass grows here with

its white, woolly flakes, rushes and tough sedges; crowberry and bog mulberry, Lapp bramble with its large, astringent, red berries; birches, one finger high, sprawl over the ground; everywhere it yields under

Finmarken

the foot, look out, cling to the weathered stone. And where does it lead to further? Well, as a matter of fact, nowhere, this somehow is the end of the world; beyond this no roads lead, beyond this there is nothing else but a few Lapp names on the map; that anyone could live there, I don't know; because it is too depressing. And too many mosquitoes.

We drive down through a luminous night, we drive through the dwarf birches, and through the Nordic forest, and through the valley of rumbling rapids. I look—it seemed to me that dry forked twigs were lying on the ground; and instead they were cast-off reindeer antlers.

70° 40′ 11″ N.L.

But now already the North really begins; desolate, my friends, absolutely desolate, nothing but a cold sea and bare rock; here even the mountains could not grow up, they look as if their tops had been cut off; only granite floes, falling steeply into the sea, on the top a bare and slightly greenish platform, only a kind of greenish mouldiness, or something, and nothing else besides; but the styrman promises us that we may see a whale. Only the seagulls become more numerous; they swing round the boat, catch the crests of the waves in their talons and scream; they are the only beggars in the whole of the North.

So you see, so you see; at last beauty and picturesqueness are at their wits' end; how little is needed to penetrate to the bottom of the bare and austere grandeur of the world? Lord, I know that we are only a tiny planet; and on it that strange zigzag peninsula that is called Europe counts for little! But I have gazed at the stars sitting on the Greek columns in

Girgenti, I have breathed the mild, mint-like air on Montserrat; and now I snivel with a frozen nose in Sørøysund and am waiting to see whether I shall see a

whale. I know all this is not worth talking about, and others have seen a hundred times more; but I am a local patriot of Europe; and if I should never see anything more until I die I shall say: I have seen the greatness of the world. Some day perhaps our planet will grow old, or we human beings may look after it,

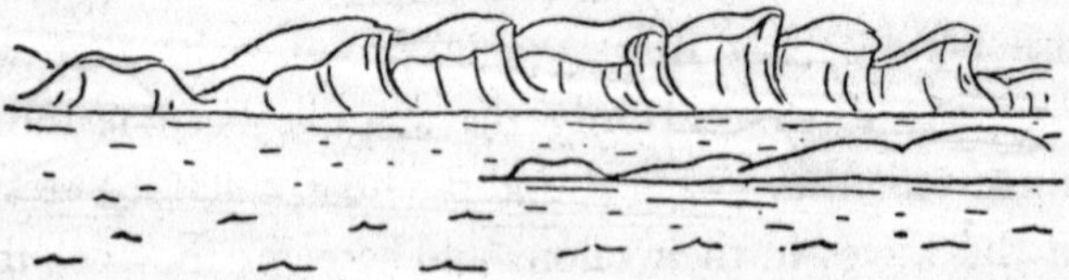

and make such a mess of the world that there will not even be any sea-gulls to cry over the waters; but even if we cut ourselves into little bits, we could not injure the greatness of the world. I know that that is no material comfort; we live in evil times, and our hearts are cramped with worry; but the world is great.

* * * * *

"The most northerly town in Europe is Hammerfest": so we learned at school, and it happens to be true; but it is also true that just behind Hammerfest

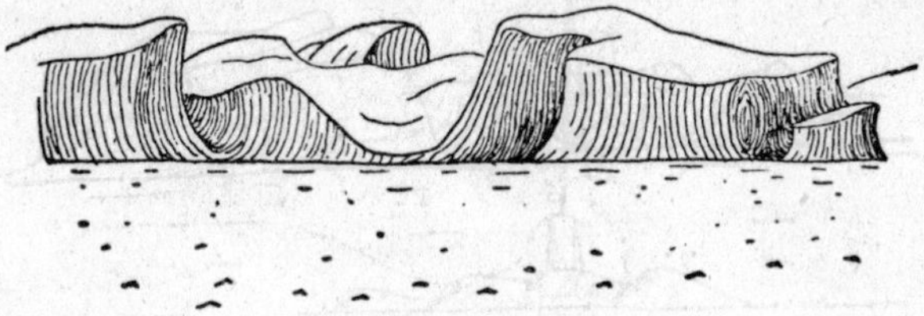

Sørøysund

is the most northerly forest in Europe (it is a handful of dwarf birches), and that the largest building in the town, even in the whole of Norway, from Trondheim to Nordkapp, is the local lunatic asylum; this prompts one to think that local life probably has its seamy side,

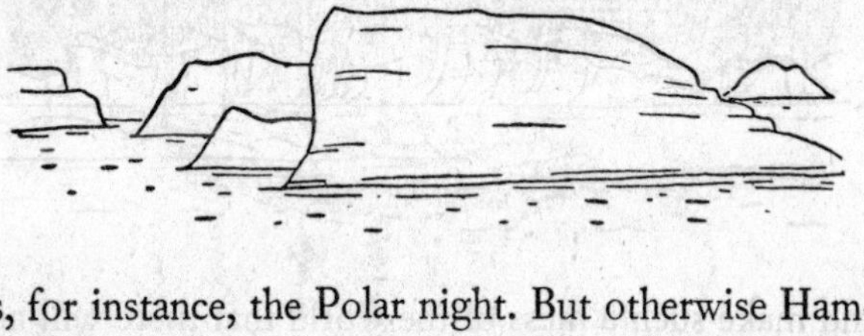

as, for instance, the Polar night. But otherwise Hammerfest is not very different from Tromsø, or Harstad, or other towns from Bergen up; it is built as much of wood as they are, and it is as clean, it has two or three streets shaded with telegraph poles, in every little house there is a shop with tobacco, chocolate, china, and postcards—here the shops with victuals contain nothing but tins; in every window they have cactuses (particularly of the genera *Cereus and Echinopsis*),

Hammerfest

and mothers take little children about on a lead, and this on the whole is all that the roaming eye of the wanderer falls across here. If he takes a couple of steps more the town remains behind him, and round about are only rocks and rocks; here and there a cushion of mountain catch-fly, a bluebell, or saxifrage, and below

the grey sea murmurs and sobs; and then there is nothing but bare and uninhabited islands. This, then, is the most northerly town in Europe. Where already farming comes to an end, fishermen can still survive;

and where fishing comes to an end, shopkeepers, export-agents, cashiers still obtain a foothold. I tell you, the most northerly sign of life is business; and human progress will not cease until on the North Pole there will be a wooden shack with postcards, tobacco, and knitted gloves; and one or two cashiers will find a livelihood there as well.

* * * * *

Besides that there is (to wit, in Hammerfest) a large and excellent harbour; the entire white *Stella Polaris* was at anchor there, and boats from the White Star and Cunard Line, a French gunboat, grey and bare, and a big black collier from Svalbard, from which they were just unloading coal, Finnish boats with wood, little whaling steamers with a little gun in the bows, motor fishing boats, launches, sailing boats, and barges; it is strange, when one sails on the ocean, a strong spirit of fellowship springs up in one with all the boats he meets, whether it be a case of a fifty thousand ton ocean liner, or a tossing barge with herrings; he simply must wave to them, and wish them a happy journey. Perhaps it has got into people's blood. and that is why a motor-driver waves his greetings to a cyclist, a pedestrian to a motor-driver; on firm land people also meet here with dignity and friendliness, like the boats on the open sea.

"A nice boat," we used to say like an expert, if we met one like the *Stella Polaris* or the *Bremen*, but we only greeted her with a sort of polite detachment; after all, you would not force yourself upon such swells; it is better, I say, to keep them away from the body a bit. But when we were passing a rolling barge or an eager motor-boat, snorting from one island to another, we nearly fell overboard through throwing our arms about and waving our caps in greeting. A pleasant

journey, brave little boat from Lofoten; hello, little steamer from Öksfjord; we smaller fry must stick together on every sea.

NORDKAPP

But now already it is really rather rough; it is blowing furiously, and every other moment a strong tide is swaying the *Håkon* on to its side. It makes you laugh; you try to cross the deck and step out briskly, and of its own self the deck lifts itself willingly to your foot; you try to place your foot on the ground, but the deck recedes and you have the stupid feeling of falling as if in the dark you can't see the step and tread into the void. But who for whatever reason has already staggered with a giddy foot on the uncertain surface of the earth feels at home in a moment. I think that the best preventative against sea-sickness is a bottle of cognac; you must, of course, drink it empty on dry land and then practise walking; and you acquire experience which one day may come in useful to you on board. In a masterly manner you will balance, and stagger, and seek ground under your feet; your head will turn, and you will cling to the captain, ropes, and

railings, but in your soul you will feel grand and exhilarated, and you will sing and shout, while down in the cabins the teetotaler souls will moan and murmur prayers prescribed for the hour of death. *Probatum est.*

The shores of primeval schist are bare and dark; on top it has been planed by the Ice Age into a surface like a table, and it falls down to the sea black and steep; a terribly austere region is this, but it has style and greatness that is almost tragic. All the time, one wall after another, a bare mountain plateau without end, cut across by steep gorges, pallid with lichen, and mouldy with lowly vegetation. It is a ghastly melancholy; one is not even astonished when all of a sudden the *Håkon Adalstein* begins to scurry straight towards a black wall of rock; most probably it is suicide, the captain stands in an open black coat with his hands in his pockets, and he only blinks to himself, a small, black officer on the bridge mutters between his teeth "*Stödig, stödig.*"

"*Stödig,*" repeats the man at the helm, and gazes with blue eyes at the dark rock. Now only eleven

yards; that rock isn't bad, but in front of it rather disagreeable black cliffs protrude from the surf. Well, what?

"*Hart bagboard,*" says the dark officer.

"*Hart bagbord,*" repeats the man at the helm, and turns the wheel; the *Håkon Adalstein* blew a hoarse blast on the siren, and suddenly there was a whirling on the rock like a white blizzard; thousands, ten thousands of screaming seagulls circled round the rock, and only now did one notice how many there were still sitting on every ledge; they looked like porcelain insulators on the roof of the telephone exchange. The boat hooted again, and then whole banks of white seagulls flew up and circled like snowflakes round the dark rock. This then is Fugleberg, or the birds, mountain.

"And what do the poor things live on here?" a compassionate voice enquired anxiously at my side.

Well, on what; perhaps on fish.

"That's dreadful," the compassionate voice sighed. "Poor fish!" And still one rock after the other, they all looked alike, all equally hopelessly bare, and austere like the last one. The *Håkon Adalstein* gave a long blow, and headed straight for that vertical, black wall.

"Fugleberg again?"

"Ne-ei. Nordkapp."

So look at that, Nordkapp. You might say that this Europe ends somewhat suddenly, as if chopped off; and rather sadly. Admittedly, it is like a black margin. If you approached it from the North you might say: Good Lord, what sad and big island is this?—Well, it is such a strange country of cares, they call it Europe; it might be a paradise on earth, but deuce take it, somehow it doesn't work; hence that wall of rock as a warning here. As a matter of fact it is not really the most northerly point in Europe; that is on that low and extended cliff over there, which is called Knivskjærodden, that means a knife; and altogether the most northerly point of the continent is further away over there on Nordkyn, while Nordkapp is only the end of the island of Magerøy. But that's all the same; Europe chose Nordkapp for her northernmost point; she thinks that if it's the end, then at any rate it should be worth it. She always liked to show off a

Nordkap

bit; so at least she pretends to a more showy end than she really does possess.

The end of Europe; over there it is true, behind that white sea there are still the Bear Islands, and Svalbard, but one no longer takes these so seriously. Yes, an end; so simply, and abruptly, with such a big, and unemotional exclamation mark, our continent comes to an end with all its history, with something so primeval and original as this wall of rock. I know one day, there will be a huge inscription on it—SHELL, or FYFFE'S, or something; but for the present it stands here clean, great and serious as at the beginning of the world. Oh no, this is not the end of Europe; it is her beginning. The end of Europe is down there below among men, where they are at their busiest.

Slowly, slowly, the *Håkon Adalstein* skirts the black rock and drops anchor in Hornvik bay; they will catch fish so that there will be some change from the tinned Trondheim food. Anyone who likes can hold on to the extremely long line until suddenly the line starts to run out, and he begins to shout that he has caught something; and the sailor comes running up, and winds up on board a silvery fish, as heavy as a young pig, and as toothy as a crocodile; or a blue and speckled sea trout; or a very beautiful little fish which, however, is not good for eating. Any passenger who doesn't catch anything feels slightly offended and declares that he has been given a bad place where there are no fish. In this fishing, as after all, in some other circumstances of life, women act with great passion. I know a compassionate lady who on the *Håkon Adalstein* hauled in the line with so much energy that I said to her: "Poor fishes!"

For a moment she stopped pulling, but then she let the rod fall still lower. "I am catching only the rapacious ones," she said. "Look what a fish that Swedish Greta has caught!"

* * * * *

With the evening the wind and waves have settled, but instead, clouds have extended all over Hornvika; a long sharp serpentine we climb up on to Nordkapp. In the first turn of the path the engineer sits down on a stone, and cannot go any further; he wipes his pale eyes, and grins with embarrassment, while even the two decrepit ladies from the *Håkon* climb upwards. So you see, old chap; for twenty years you have been sailing round here in the ship's engine-room, and only because of that you came here to see it really for once; well and to Nordkapp you will most probably never get. One would not say so, only a thousand feet high, and what a struggle; above one is gripped by storm and cloud, but it isn't a cloud, but specks of ice, and now you have to force your way through fog along a bare, stony plain, you cannot see its end, nor edge; and the styrman promised us that we should see the midnight sun! But even up here a tiny dryas creeps between the stony ruins, mountain catch-fly completes its flowering, the moss saxifrage cringes; except for that only a whisp of sedge, and cotton-grass, raw and shivering bog, pale lichen, and nothing but that bare ruin. The end of the world. And then out of the mist a wooden hut appears, and in front of it—I can't help it, but it really is a dance floor; and a concertina plays in the hut; I know, it is dreadful, but besides, there is a whole boat-load of Americans. What do they want here after all? The end of Europe, that's our affair; let them go and have a look at the end of America, if there is one; and if there isn't, let them make one for themselves.

The clouds roll by one after the other, from close to they are ugly, bedraggled misty rags; you can't see five yards ahead, you squeeze up against the sides of the hut and zealously tremble with cold. Suddenly the

mist opens up a bit, and a thousand feet below, under your feet, glistens an opal, shining sheet of sea; there below the sun is shining. And then everything again is enveloped in masses of cloud, it is hopeless; only towards the North does it begin to glow yellow, and bright, the streaming tatters of cloud dissolve into gold, and again nothing; only a new gust of icy specks whip your face. Well, even this has a beauty of its own, says the pilgrim (to keep the conversation going); sombre, it is true, and raw, but isn't it the North? And then in the West the sky reveals a green and cold little pool of azure; the clouds tear apart; suddenly a terrible light streams out there, it extends like a huge rainbow bubble; the dark scenery of the precipices above the mother-of-pearl sea is revealed—and one cliff after another begins to burn with a heavy, coppery glow. And now it is here: all of a sudden a vast golden sky as far as the horizon, and quite low in the North, just above the line of the sea, like a tiny red-hot gimlet, a strange, red sun pierces the sky. It is so small that it almost gives one a shock; poor thing, after all, you are only a star! The thin, fiery blade of the sun cuts across the golden mirror of the sea; only right on the horizon, directly and infinitely to the North, fierce and green shines an icy white line. Here the pilgrim can look straight into the face of the sun without blinking; so you are the sun, you small red star. I know, perhaps one day you will look like this after millions of years, when you begin to shrink and to grow old and cold; but the silene will still flower, and the tiny white knot-grass will raise its mallets, but what will it be like with us then, I don't know; do you think that man will be no loss? It is true, we are only standing at the end of Europe; who would think immediately of the end of the world?

And the big styrman comes up and points with his heavy paw towards the midnight sun. "I promised it to you, and you thought that I was lying. Well here it is."

Yes, here it is; we have seen the midnight sun, and now we may go home; we have seen the end and the beginning, and the fiery blade pointing straight, and austere like the angel's sword; never, never, man, will the gates of paradise open. Well what is one to do.

The sky will become covered with grey-gold tatters, the storm will rage, the world will take on its covering of mist, and the icy specks will strike the faces of the chilly sons of Adam. Children, children, it's time to go home.

THE JOURNEY BACK

I could no longer trace it with my finger on the map;

I don't know exactly which way we sailed, and where we anchored; wait a bit, it was Honningsvåg, one of the most forsaken human habitations in the world, and then again Hammerfest, and Kvalsund, where we landed at zero hour, and not even the children and perhaps nobody was asleep, such a terribly white, such a ghastly clear daylight there was; and then came Vargsund, as smooth as oil, and again Tromsø, but it is not that that muddles me; it was the sky, and the sea, those changing, and endless days without dusk nights or dawns; there time is abolished, that's all. There time doesn't flow, but it is spilt, without banks like a sea; and it mirrors in itself the course of the sun and the pilgrimage of the clouds, but it does not progress with them, and does not flow away; here only the watch on the wrist with needless eagerness, and ridiculous tick, measures the time that does not exist. It is as strange and confusing as if space were distorted and there were no difference between above and below;

one might even grow accustomed to this, but at the beginning one feels as little at home in it as in another world.

Tenderly, with golden obliquity the sunshine glides over the round shoulders and the steep brows of the mountain; it may be two o'clock in the morning, or five in the afternoon, it is just the same, and in fact, my friend, it does not matter; you sleep, or you don't sleep, that also does not matter when for once you are beyond time. Even the food on the boat will not take you away from the immutability of time; all the time *smørgås*, and again *smørgås*, all the time salt meat and fish, and brown goat's cheese with syrup, whether it is breakfast, supper, or dinner; I let my watch run down, and I let day, year, and century, slip out of my mind; what use is it for man to know the minute or hour if he lives in eternity?

Here there is no night, and there is not even day; here are only the morning hours, when the sun is still low, all golden with the dawn and silvery with the

dew, the fine, sparkling sun of early day; and then without a break came the hours of late afternoon, when the sun is already low, turning gold with the sunset, already purple and misty with the sweet melancholy

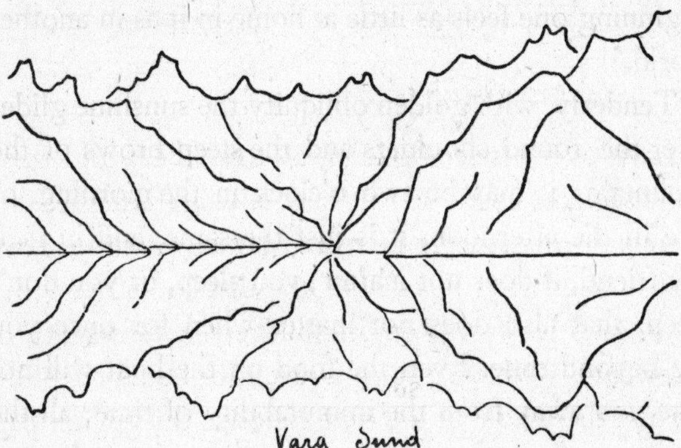

of evening. It is only morning without beginning passing over into evening without end, and never does the high bright arch of the steep noon raise its vault aloft, and the golden evening without an end in the fiery midnight dissolves into the silvery morning without a beginning, and it is again day: a Polar day, an enormous day, a day spun out of nothing but its first and last hours.

I know in all places there are beautiful hours; never mind, such a sunset in its brocade glory, such

a dawn over a sleeping land, all over the world there are moments, well, it's no use talking; but they are merely fleeting, not to be retained, moments too short, and in a quarter of an hour the display is over. But here, in Stjernfjord, on Lopphavet, in Grøtsund, or elsewhere, we have a sunset which for hours is golden for us; the whole of the time it floods the greater part of the sky and of the sea, already the whole of the West and North have blazed up, already the East is catching fire, already over there the dawn begins in the morning glow; and now sea and sky become merged into something immensely glorious and strange: at one and the same time it is a radiant dusk

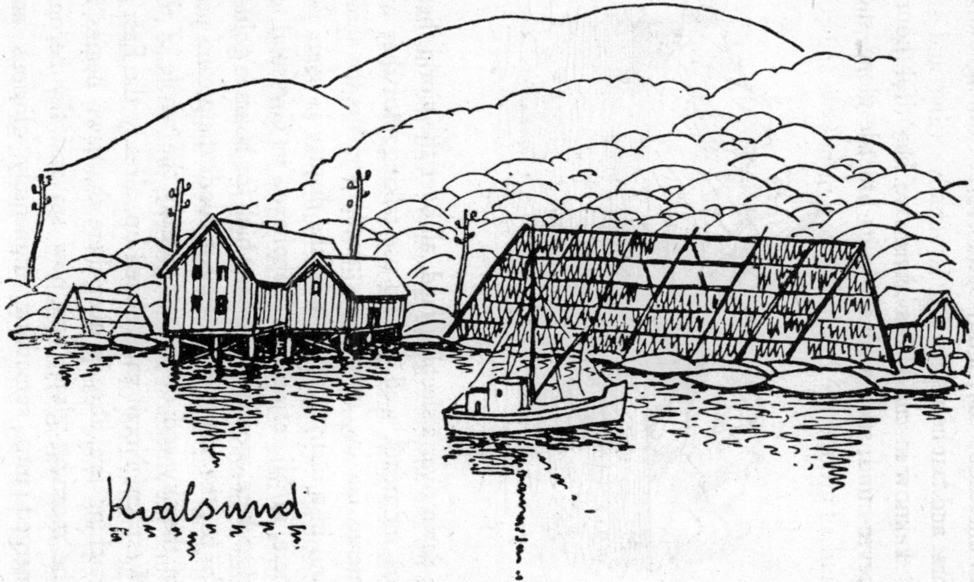
Kvalsund

and a pale dawn; the impassioned sunset filters through a chilly dawn, beyond the blue crest of the mountains the fiery disc of the sun is already rising and still setting, the scarlet smoothness of the evening sea begins to sparkle with the silver ripples of morning, and all around the bright horizon turns pale and cold

with the austere feast of the dawn. And the sun halts over Gabaon, and the desperate call of Faust is fulfilled: the moment stands still that is so beautiful, and it spreads without limit in the sublimity of space and time. Where have you got to, man! Don't you see that it is another world, and where already another, great and terrible order is valid? Yes, I know: without limit the duration of the moment, and without end the annihilation of time.

God, where was it then, where were we then! Let us say, it was in Malangen, and that small harbour was called Målsnes, but that is immaterial, it was somewhere in the universe; just before midnight there was a short drizzle of rain but then the clouds flared up like fluttering brazen torches, and they rose above the indigo helmets of the mountains; and the setting sun appeared above the golden sea, and its terrible, thin, fiery blade pierced the sheet from North to South; then the summits of the mountains began to glow out

from the olive and blue shadows with pink heat, above a tiny harbour, sunk into the depths of the evening, a midnight rainbow raised its bright arch, the mountains became transfixed in great and glorious conflagration, the blood-red rocks, and above them the glistening snow, it was like a Eucharist, it was like the elevation of the Host, and the sun, almost nothing but a fiery point in the furthest horizon, struck the Nordic midnight hour. Then from the engine-room an old marine engineer, square-jawed and sparing of words, clambered up, spat into emerald water of the harbour, and mumbled as he descended again to the machines.

By special grace, yes, by quite special favour and

generosity, we were granted such a blessed sun, as well as an abundance of cloud, and mist, and rainbows, and showers; yes, we have seen something of everything; we have sailed through arcades of rainbows, and in the night-time we ran into milky mist so that we could hardly drag ourselves along, hooting and

sounding the alarm, we saw the peaks of the mountains floating above the white clouds, the heels of the rocks cut off by the overcast sky, which fell upon the water like a damp sack, and mountain ranges waving little plumes of clouds, smoking like volcanoes of mist, misty like breath on transparent chalcedony, the skies in all their glory, and the grey sea soaked with rain, blue, purple, a sea melted into gold, changing, and iridescent like soap, metallic waters, mother-of-pearl waters and silky ones, silent and spiky waters, and thank God, there was enough of it; behind quiet and cheerful Ofotfjord already lay Narvik, the end of the voyage.

It was enough, and we sampled everything; but I should like to travel the same way once more; I should still like to see the night here. The night which has no end. Without end the black sky, and the sea, the twinkling little lighthouses and blinking buoys, the tiny red and white lights, the shining human windows in the fog, the lights in the harbours, the moon above the icy mountains, the fisherman's lantern, and the stars sparkling in the frosty night; the dark end of Europe projecting into black and endless darkness. That must be sad, Lord, that must be sad! But as if there were little sadness anywhere in the world, and as if we were not here to try to bear it? We have sampled everything, but it was only from the bright side; how little one knows, great little Norwegian land, how little one knows who has not yet learned to know everything!

NARVIK

Narvik, that is a harbour, and at the same time the terminus of the most northerly railway in the world (except for the Murmansk railway, but I don't count that because I haven't been there); it subsists on ore from Kiruna, on Swedish timber, and Norwegian herrings; besides that, it is the intersection of four fjords, and the meeting-place of a whole circle of high mountains, like the Sleeping Queen, Harjangsfjellene, and other famous peaks, crowned with ice, and more noble perhaps than anywhere else. It cannot leave you alone: if you are somewhere among the mountains you begin to climb up them to have a closer look.

There was a cat, it ran down to meet us with its tail vertically erect, and then for half an hour it accom-

panied us into the mountains; then somewhere there was a waterfall rumbling, and the mountain pines were as superb as cathedral candelabra; that is why I have drawn a picture of them. *Empetrum Nigrum*, and *Rubus chamaemorus*, *Eriophorum vaginatum*, *Juncus*, and other boggy and peaty plants were growing there; I am referring to it so that you may see that I was in an absolutely alert state of mind. Later on down below smooth Ofotfjord reveals itself between rocky cliffs, and groves of pine, and above, on the cupolas of the mountains, the snow fields shimmer without end; but for man this is not enough, and he says to himself that he must still have a look behind that rocky spur over there, and then still a bit further up; and so it chanced that I discovered the place where I went lost.

It was only an exposed plateau of huge bare boulders, as easy to survey as the palm of the hand; here and there a tiny peaty pool, here and there a creeping bunch of juniper, birch, or blue willow (*Salix Lapponum*); and nothing more, only higher up the shining glaciers, and one rock as steep and fantastic as the Matterhorn; and I sat down on a boulder above the peaty lake so that I could draw it. I can produce witnesses who saw me drawing; and all of a sudden I was missing; the simple fact was that suddenly the boulder had no one on it. Every man is slightly odd, and sensible people allow him some sort of momentary whim; but when at the end of five minutes I did not appear again to be sitting on that boulder and sketching, it began to strike them as queer, and they set out to shout and search; and only then did it become clear that I really had got lost. They searched for me among the boulders, for the first hour alive, and for the second only as a corpse; and when they did not find me it was almost a certainty that I had fallen into that little lake, and sunk into the bottomless peat, or something, and they ran to Narvik to

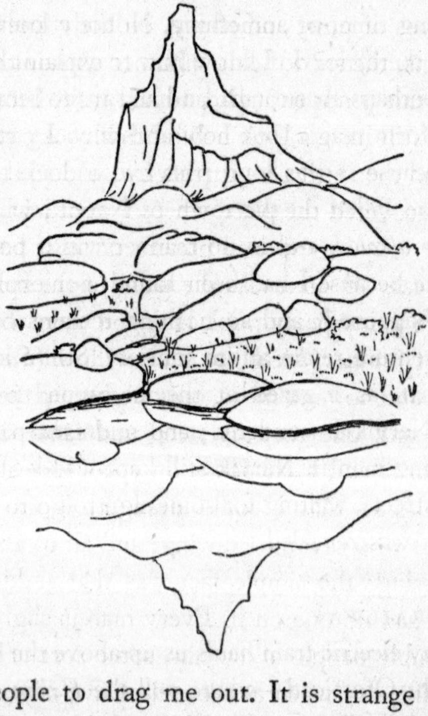

fetch people to drag me out. It is strange that we human beings demand for everything a rational, or natural explanation; here in the mountains of Norway, you know, people often get lost, and not even one of their buttons is found. The Lapps say that a mountain has taken them in. Only after an hour's march did they find me up above Narvik, sitting by the road-side and stroking the cat, pulling its proud tail, and holding in my hand a live mouse that pussy had retrieved for me. According to them I only raised my astonished eyes, and mumbled something like keeping me waiting for a long time, or something. Nobody knew how I had got there, nor do I know how to explain the whole affair; perhaps that cat had a hand in it, because cats can perform magic, but how and why, I cannot tell. And because it was long past five o'clock a terrible curse had fallen on the town of Narvik, which they call *ikke alkohol*, and in no manner was it possible to celebrate because I had been found, nor explain how it had happened; and so nothing remains but to let my adventure retain all its sobriety. Still a long time after that, as I gazed at the ice-capped mountains above Narvik I wondered; and midnight passed and the young men in Narvik still kept wandering in the bright streets, waiting for some sign to go to bed; but no sign was revealed.

OFOT RAILWAY

A tiny electric train hauls us up above the final inlet of bright Ofotfjord—where will the *Håkon Adalstein* be now! Well, most likely it is loafing around the Lofoten harbours; everywhere on the brygge of the harbour our dog is already waiting, and inquisitively wagging his heavy tail. It is only now that one remembers—in fact, we were good friends, all those on board the *Håkon;* no one even gave it a thought, and yet it happened; we did not perhaps exchange a single word during the whole of the journey, and only glanced at one another from time to time; well, and yet everyone came to shake hands with emotion when

the moment of parting arrived. Let that be, it was a good boat; it still should carry many men of all kinds of tongues; they need not even speak together, and have councils and conferences, and yet even so they may perhaps shake hands at the end of the journey.

And already only a tiny bit of Norwegian land remains; here, poor thing, from the sea to the Swedish frontier, it is not even ten miles wide; yet it is all rock, all iceberg on the top, all precipice, and waterfall below, that is Hundalen. You can hardly set up here the little guard's station, all round the horizon cupolas of ice, and peaks, at any moment a tunnel projects us into a still more barren and stonier world. Never mind, it was a fine land, the whole of Norway, and its people; and if I were to mention what was unpleasant

there I should only remember the American churches, the mosquitoes, and partial prohibition; besides that, one dish I did not care for, but that for certainty I did not taste, and so I can't tell. A good, austere land of good-natured people; a rural and small-town land, where brave people live decently and quietly in clean little boxes surrounded by the most

V

Again in Sweden

IV

Again in Sweden

—Fantastic, monumental, and sometimes almost unreal world; but already we have passed through the tunnel that forms the national frontier, and we are in Sweden. In earlier times there used to be a frontier station, but they had to abandon it because of the severe climate; then they moved a bit further into Sweden, to Vassijaure, where the climate is no longer so mountainous because it is good twenty-five feet

V

Again in Sweden

THE NORTHERN TUNDRA

—fantastic, monumental, and sometimes almost unreal world; but already we have passed through the tunnel that forms the national frontier, and we are in Sweden. In earlier times there used to be a frontier station, but they had to abandon it because of the severe climate; then they moved a bit further into Sweden, to Vassijaure, where the climate is no longer so mountainous because it is good twenty-five feet lower. You notice that at once: here already boulders, dark bogs, and steely lakes abound; in fact, it forms a huge terrace of boulders, piled up between the mountain ramparts and falling steeply down to the sea. Among the primary rocks only a little wisp of rushes, or of cotton-grass, a few dwarf birches, and nothing else besides; but further down the road slopes towards Abisko, the tundra increases, and endless brushwood of birch curls up between the peaks and into it penetrates the endless lake of Torneträsk, spangled with green islets; and we are in the very centre of Lappland. Of course, from the train you do not expect to see natural Lapp settlements with reindeer and other native charms; but when instead one comes across Lapps (in national costumes) selling foreign souvenirs, and Lapp women (in national costumes) as maids in spotlessly clean, red Swedish houses, one is rather taken aback, and one says to one's self that folk-lore picturesqueness is in a bad way in the world, if as almost everywhere where one has met it, it is a sign either of the tourist industry or of a servile relationship towards people far less pictorial and obviously better off; it seems as if in this world original costumes, and other ethnological peculiarities now only belong to people who in this way earn their livelihood. Of course, it can't go on like this, and already now, but with certainty, I mourn the decline of this small portion of terrestrial beauty, and dignity that is called folk-lore.

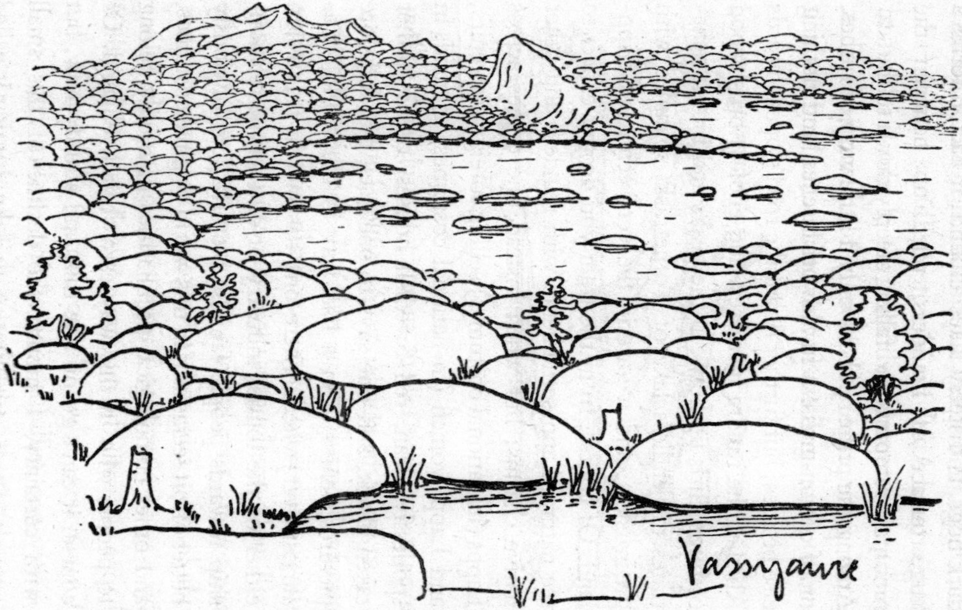
Vassijaure

On the other hand, Nature, I hope, will retain for a bit longer its original Lapp character; partly because here around Abisko it is protected like a natural park, perhaps lest someone might get it into his head to grow sugar cane and have coffee plantations here, and to some small extent also because nothing else will

ever grow here except tundra of birch and willow (apart from the smaller weeds, which I could not very clearly discern from the train). As for the mountains, the position is no longer so certain with them; people will find something in them that can be used to make armaments, or what not, and then they will load the whole mountains on to wagons and transport them by way of Narvik to Krupp's or Armstrong's, as has happened with the mountain which used to be called Kirunavaara; now it's no longer a mountain but simply 700 millions tons of first quality iron ore. I have drawn it, together with lake Luossajärvi, in which it is reflected; but the town of Kiruna, with its standardized, red workmen's cottages, and with all the social, humanitarian, and other achievements of modern industry, in the midst of a tragic green desert of tundra, there was no room for that town in my picture.

And so without end or limit the Arctic tundra

slowly but definitely passes over into the Northern forest: at first nothing but stones, and low bushes, here and there the stump of a birch tree, and dry wood, here and there the golden sparkle of cinquefoil, or whatever it is (it might be *Sibbaldia procumbens*); then the underwood continues to become thicker, it is taller and shaggier, everywhere, as far as the eye can see, the white little flames of birch stems, mingling with them slim and glistening aspens, dark bushes of alders, and silvery willows, and everywhere beneath the willows, beneath the crowberries, beneath the birches surges the peat, nothing but black, wet, shining peat. And then above the low undulating growth a dried and twisted stem raises itself and carries a meagre crown; the shaggy brushwood of knotted pines begins to darken; strangely our mountain knee-pine is absent, here only the tall, pathetic pine struggles tenaciously for life. And now already it has won the battle; it is still gnarled, and tattered by the storms, and broken by the snow, but already its lanky stem and heavy boughs give a steep and solemn character to the whole country. The birches are becoming fewer, the pines are gaining ground; from the intensely green brambles, from the creeping junipers, the first austere stumps and stems of the firs protrude, like masts, whipped by the wind into the most peculiar brooms, besoms and spiky cudgels, fluttering pinions and extended arms. For a long time yet it is not a forest, it is not yet a collective vegetation; every tree wrestles alone with the elements, with the soil, every one differently formed, differently branded, and wounded by its own fate; it is not a forest but a huge field of battle and a camp of warriors each fighting for himself. What can one do, where the struggle for life is hardest everyone of us is thrown upon our own resources; show yourself what you can do and what you can stand. A hard life it is, but how many adventures all the same; and you will meet trees, nothing but a battered cossack, nothing but an old and experienced campaigner; this one gaunt like Don Quixote, that one lacerated like a Japanese fighter; a sinewy tall fellow, all scars and knuckles, a wounded

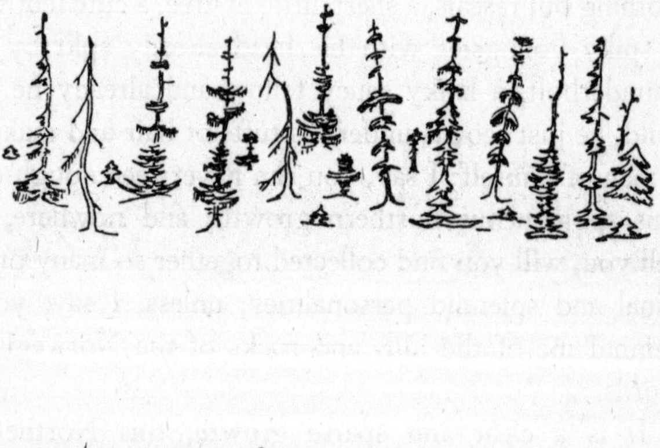

invalid raising to the sky the stumps of terrifying limbs, a swaggering and thick-set braggart, a poor hungry devil beaten down from all sides, such an unlucky fellow, but still he keeps his head above water; gnarled cronies, nothing but bone, everything just hangs on them, well, and you see, they didn't give in; who would have said it of such close-tongued ones as that! God Almighty, you have got together here a fine army against the North; beneath their feet nothing but rascals, a sharp little fir-tree, a cute fellow, a spiky youngster with his head already split by a thunderbolt, a lanky saucy fellow and already he is wild, he just scowls under his tufts of hair and makes a man of himself; I say, you can never see enough of this spontaneous northern growth; and nowhere, I tell you, will you find collected together so many original and splendid personalities; unless, I say, you remind me of the hills and rocks of the Norwegian fjords.

It is a clear and sparse growth, this Northern margin of the woods, but what weathered fellows, what pillars, what shaggy ones draped with mossy wadding! Everywhere there is the gleam of little dark pools, everywhere abound piles of black stones, everywhere tufts of wiry grass, and the dense fleece of brambles; glistening ferns shine out with their fine, bright little flames. Slowly, slowly the Nordic tundra lines up into a sparse forest of fir-tree masts, and of the noble cathedral cupolas of the pines; there are some trees that you will remember to the day of your death, like some human faces; there are some trees that are almost sacred. And then suddenly a broad clearing springs out among them, a fresh and naked clearing,

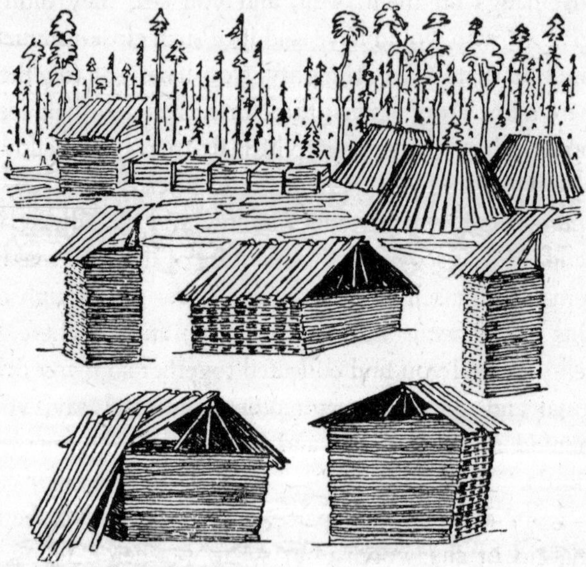

shining with felled trunks, one glade after another glowing red with willow-herb and billowing with carroty grass; with the Northern forest the manufacture of planks and beams also begins; and here broad *älvs*, already flowing slowly, leisurely and endlessly bear away from the forests the inarticulate wood.

THE SWEDISH FORESTS

In fact, you travel through them from the Arctic Circle right to Stockholm; for twenty, thirty hours the express is pounding South all the while through forest, nothing but forest, and what a train it is, sir: I must admit that nowhere else does one travel so well

Pikälv

and so spaciously as in Sweden. Of course, at times the trees move sideways, and form a small clearing for pastures and meadows, as they do right up in Norrbottenslän, where to keep hay the people make pleasant and funny wooden huts which look as if someone has squashed them down from above; so squeezed are they into folds, with their middles pushed broadly out. The further to the South the more spacious become the homesteads, puffed up like a clucking hen; but still all the time, down in Ångermanland, in Jämtland, they are constructed of massive golden-brown beams, and stand on little wooden

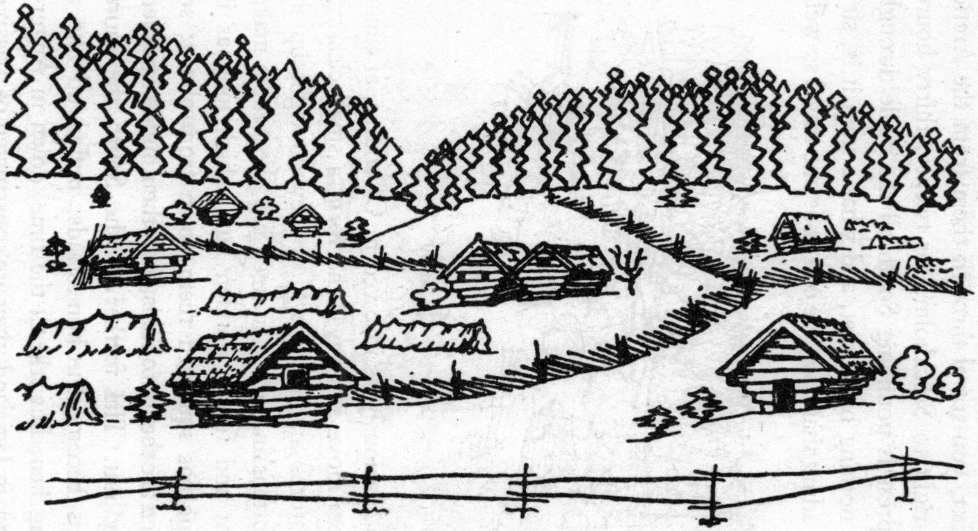

Norrbottenslän

supports as is seemly in mountain regions; only somewhere in Hälsingland does the red Sweden with white border-work begin.

And then the rivers: every moment some *älv* cuts

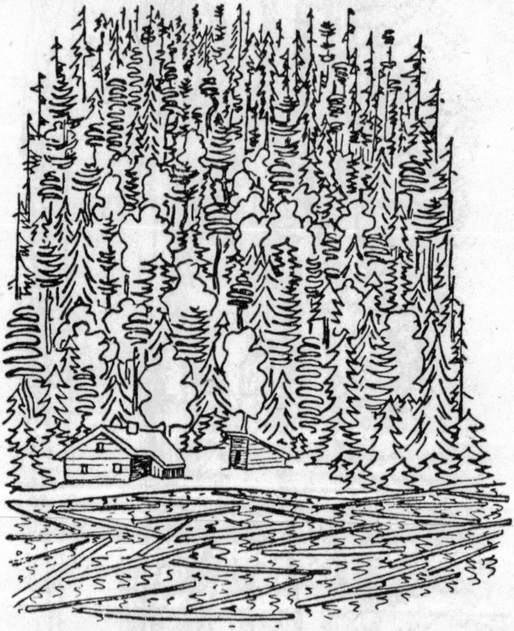

through the infinite forest; and these are rivers as broad and silent as lakes, or fresh little streams running over rapids, black and white with foam; but for the most part they are powerful, quiet, immensely serious streams, which higher up have handed over their impetuosity to the power stations, and now just in a matter-of-fact way, patiently, and rather lazily, they

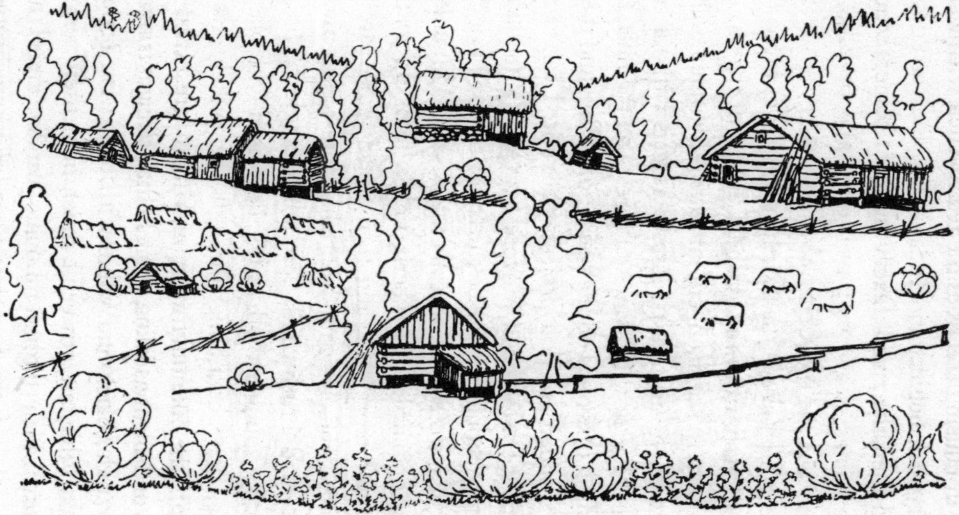

Ångermansland

bear the felled timber to the saw-mills and harbours. There you have Luleälv, and Piteälv, Åbyälv, Umeälv, and Ångermanälven, and Indalsälven, and then down to Ljusnanälven, and Dalälven, and lots of others whose names escape me; even our Labe, or Elbe, is nothing but the old Celtic *elv*.

Everything else is the Northern forest; as far as the eye can reach, from the extended ridges of the mountains down to the plain, cut into strips by innumerable *älvs*, nothing but forests, forests, forests without end or limit. The flowing waves of forests on the hills, the dark sheet of woods on the plains; only here and there a tall wooden erection projects above it. I can't say, perhaps it's a look-out for forest fires, or something. And how should I describe the forest to you? I ought to begin at the edge, but really there is no edge: unless a strip of purple willowherb, unless ferns up to the waist; one more step, and then already take care to extricate yourself again from that forest over those trunks, and brushwood, through a tangle of birch, through a young growth of firs, interlaced with blackberries, and scrambling through the prickly raspberries; you take only a step into that forest, and at once you have the feeling that a human being has never set foot in it before. Well, let's begin with undergrowth; look out, isn't it a mushroom there? It is, and what a mushroom! Look, you Swedes, I am bringing you from the forest a cap full of mushrooms and russet boletuses; in the forest I came to a spot where human foot has never trod before; that's why so many mushrooms grew there; what do you say to that? What, that they're poisonous? And that you don't eat them at all? They wouldn't be told, they said that they weren't edible mushrooms; but I can't believe that such a wise and cultured nation can pay

homage to such an inhuman superstition; I think that they only said it so that nobody would go and pick the mushrooms, because in those forests he would lose his way for certain. (I tried myself; in less than three minutes I didn't know where to put those mushrooms, but neither did I know where I had come from, and where to make for, I even forgot my own name; such thick forests they are. I wondered whether someone in times to come would find my dead body, surrounded by crowds of mushrooms that I had scattered there; but then it turned out that I was only fifty yards from the road.) One lady, I know, in other respects quite steadfast under the various strokes and

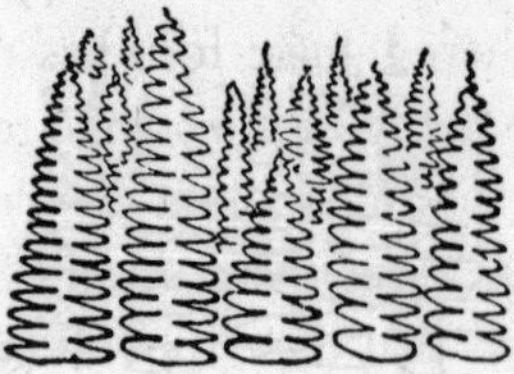

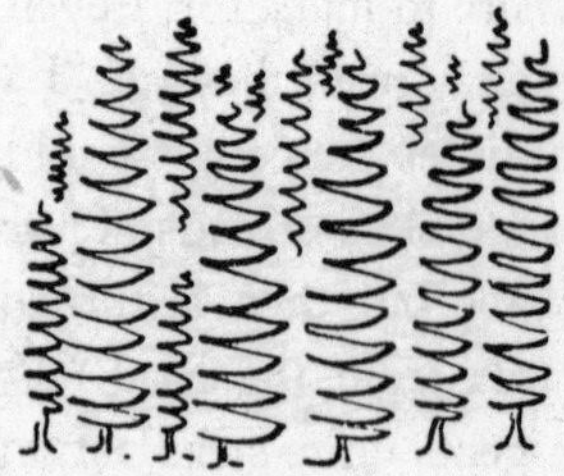

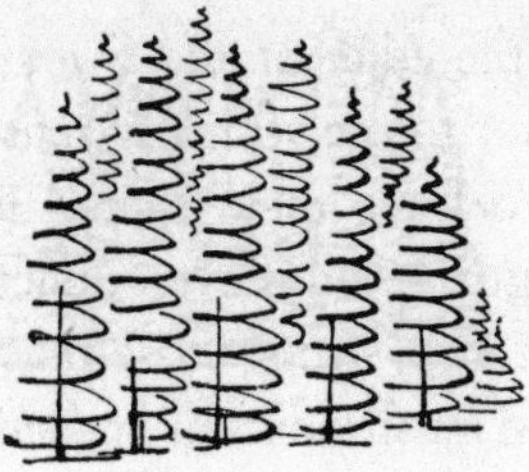

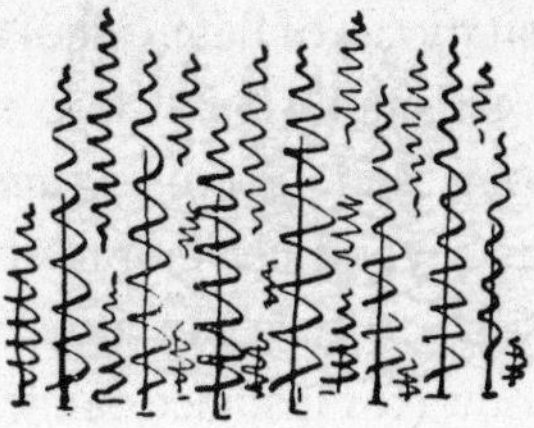

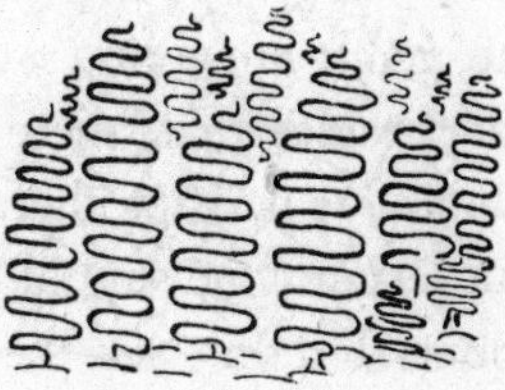

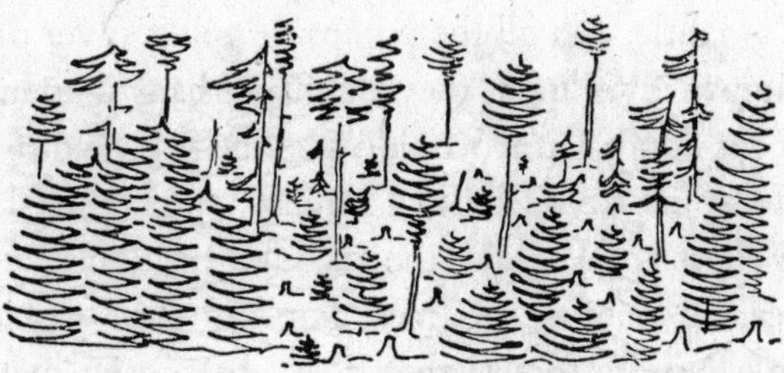

visitations of fate, who at the edge of the Swedish forest simply burst into tears: to see so many mushrooms and boletuses, and to leave them there, that was beyond her moral strength. I find it even difficult myself to turn my attention away from those mushrooms (for instance oak wood mushrooms in Småland, weathered black, and fair meadow ones in Södermanland, and the big mushrooms growing right in the ballast of the main railway in Östergötland, and those carroty boletuses!) (once I crawled through the fence of a wood after mushrooms, and a big, black horse came for me; perhaps he merely wanted to play with me, but a horse in a wood is almost a fairy creature, and besides that, there was a runic stone, and so I can't say; perhaps there was some magic behind it); but lest anyone should say that because of the mushrooms I didn't see the forest, I must make a fresh start, and it is about like this:

If you put together all the wells and brooks, all the dark pools overgrown with duck-weed, village ponds with geese, all sad puddles and sparkling gullies, all the dew drops on bents of grass and the leaves of lady's mantle, and all the pumps dripping silver drops by human dwellings, they might perhaps amount to a decent flood, but it wouldn't be the sea. And if you planted pine trees, firs and birches, spruce and larch from Paris to Warsaw, they would, no doubt, make a dreadful number of trees, but still they wouldn't make a Nordic forest; that does not consist only of those trees and expanses. Of course, such an immense collection possesses something—how am I to express it—that is elemental and immortal; but a Northern forest still has something more in it besides, some-

thing primeval, and original like a geological formation. One would say that here as it stands and lies Nature threw it up in one geological moment, as it threw up granite or spread out the chalk; and now, man, break your little stones, or cut your little sticks! And perhaps you may even destroy it, why not; but you couldn't make it, you couldn't create the Northern forest. One says a forest; it stands on millions of stems but it is one wall, one sheet, one extremely long green wave rolling south from the Arctic Circle for six hundred miles: as if up there, in the North! in the North! there were a bottomless surging spring of the immortal life and it had spread out in thundering rapids of trees, in cataracts of trees, in cascades and

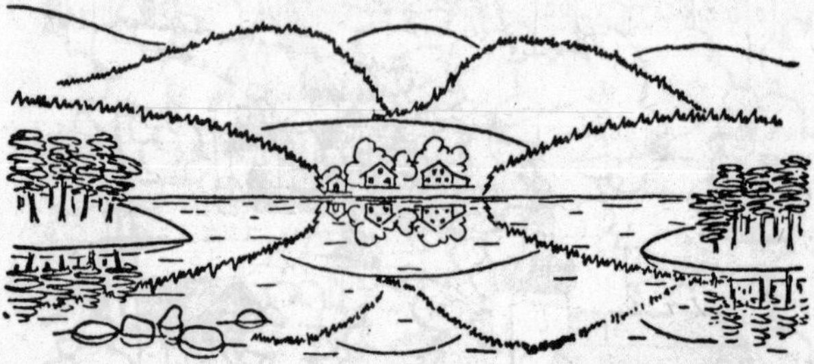

streams of trees, sprayed out in sheets, and quiet backwaters of trees always downwards, South! South! and not until here in Gästrikland, in Jämtland, beyond Dalälv does man set himself in your way with his axe, and will not let you go any further, you northern forest; except, yes, just a bit here towards Djursholm and Mälaren; these though are nothing but spinneys for the delight of the eye; but here from the South man pushes with his cows and farms against the unchained element of the Nordic forest.

OLD SWEDEN

Suecia omnis divisa est in partes duo, or the whole of Sweden, it is true, is divided into twenty-four provinces, or *län*, but in reality there are two main parts: working upwards from Öresund as far as Svealand, that is just beyond Uppland, extends the old historical

Sweden, spangled with cathedrals, forts, castles, old towns, memorials of kings, runic stones, and with historical monuments in general; but from there right up to the Arctic Circle it is spangled as a whole with

nothing but granite, waterfalls, and the Northern forest; that is the primeval Sweden.

In the historical Sweden the pilgrim's eye is at once struck by a great many churches; some of them are noble cathedrals in which the tombs of kings are to be found, of Counts Brahe, and of holy Brigits; but a cathedral like the one in Linköping, or in Lund I cannot draw for you, because it is no use, Gothic should be carved in stone, otherwise it is not the thing. Besides that, in Lund they have a very fine Norman crypt, festooned with many legends and historical stories of the giant Finn and his wife; I regret to say that I don't know Swedish, and I did not understand a word of what the local guide was saying about her; I only know what I saw. I also saw the famous cloister Vreta in the middle of a sweet graveyard; I have drawn that church so that you may see that churches too are also built like peasant farmyards, of nothing but added portions, the Lord's sheds, stables and wood-lofts, in all sorts of ways leaning against and crowding round the main farm building of the divine word. But for the most part it was the small village churches, projecting everywhere from the ancient oaks, lime, and ash trees, from the curly green of the bird-cherry trees and willows, with their turrets, gables, roofs, cupolas, and onions; I have drawn a whole collection of them, from some, finely pointed like a spindle, to those typical, broad and low, Swedish cupolas which look more like firemen's helmets or civilian bowler hats. Sometimes a Swedish church denies itself even a complete tower, and erects only a wooden belfry: altogether, the churches here sit down spaciously, civilian-like, and comfortably on the open, honest palm of the world, and do not force by any vainglorious and pathetic means their way to heaven; that must be the work of that spirit of sober and human Protestantism.

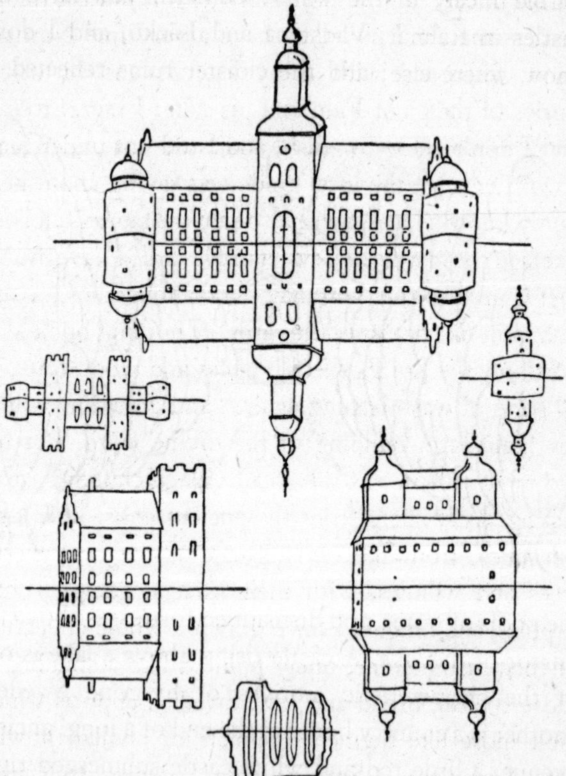

Here the forts and castles usually rise above quiet sheets of lakes; it seems to me that they do so more for the beautiful reflections than because of security from assault in feudal times; that is why they crowned their towers and round bastions with all the turrets, cupolas, lanterns and domes, so that they would mirror nicely in the water. Of such you have the castles at Kalmar, Vadstena and Läckö, and I don't know where else; and the cloister ruins reflected in

the pools of water, and dismantled fortresses above the mirror of the lake. A castle rising above a lake is one of the characteristic motives of by-gone Sweden; another is a country house at the end of a long, ancient avenue, a little red and white castle submerged right up to the roof in close-grown little park. Swedish democracy did not abolish the aristocracy, it merely let it die out, something in the manner of the elks, or ermines, that is, tactfully and with pious but helpless sympathy.

And lastly historical Sweden is thickly set with runic stones, and barrows of granite boulders. Sometimes one thinks that it is only a landmark between Lindström and Lindberg meadows, and instead it is a runic stone over which the archaeological heart may rejoice. And in places the funeral stones are arranged

into a complete circle, or in the shape of a Viking ship; in places a huge block of granite is placed like a roof above two stones to form a shelter for the corporal remains of some primeval Larsen; and the modern visitor wanders round the barrow, and wonders how the men of those times could manage to raise such a whacking, huge boulder. I have drawn for you one of those barrows, which stands by the main road just outside Trälleborg; it is strange what dignity and mystery such a witness of the past, as one calls them, gives to the country. What is the good; the greatness, and remoteness, of time fill men with the same respectful amazement as the vastness of the space. You could not imagine the amount of silver paper cartons and film wrappings that lie around such a sacred spot; I think that everyone who travels this way must photograph at that barrow his wife leaning with one hand against the prehistoric stone, with the other tidying the hair which the Baltic breeze is teasing. ("But wait, my hair is untidy," objects the *fru;* but "that doesn't matter" assures the husband, quickly pressing the catch; and there is one more family relic in the world.)

In addition to ancient monuments historical Sweden abounds in clean little towns, red farms, and ancient trees; but these I shall now keep for my next chapter.

THE LAND OF THE GOTHS

Yes, I have kept the old trees and meadows, woods, granite, and lakes until the moment when I shall have to say good-bye to the countries of the North; for the most beautiful of them after all is the North, or Nature, Nature more green than anywhere else, abounding with water, brimming over with meadows and trees, sparkling with dew, and mirroring the skies, pastoral and plentiful, the mild and blessed Nature of the North. I have kept the red, white-edged farms, and the herds of the black and white cows, the ditches full of spiraea in bloom, silvery willows and dark junipers, the granite knolls of Södermanland, and the long-drawn, curly waves of the Småland hills for the fertile and clear composure of Skåne. It is nothing, I say, nothing, but it is beautiful; I would like rather to stroke it than to describe it. It is nothing: an islet, for

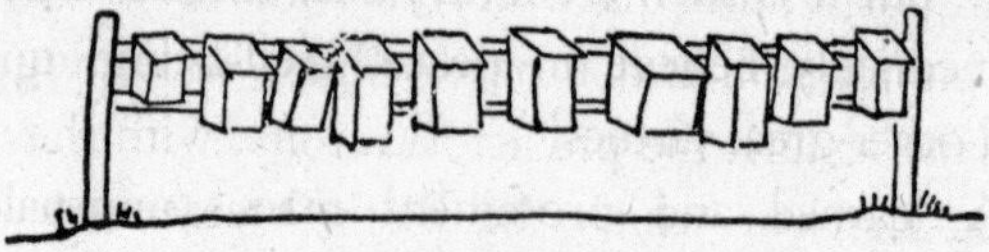

instance, reflected in the peaceful water; then why does it look like an island of the blessed? It is nothing but piebald cows ruminating in the shadow of an ancient lime; it is like a picture by an old Dutch artist who must have had a terrible liking for cows

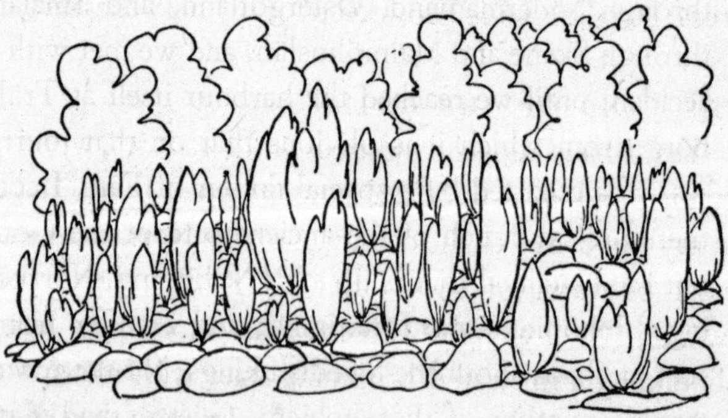

and trees. Or it is just a stone bridge over a silent river; but as if that bridge were leading to the other side, you know, the other side, where there is no longer haste, or care, and where even perhaps there is no death. Or it is only a little red and white house among the green trees; well, and one feels that one would have to be happy in it if one had one's living there; I know that it is not so easy to be happy, and that one will not learn it, perhaps not even in paradise; but it is such a country that the traveller might immediately believe in peace, well-being, quietude, and other great virtues.

A learned and prominent man, unusually well acquainted with the North, took us this way; with one hand he held the wheel of his Ford car, and with the other he pointed out to us, and outlined the archaeology, history, inhabitants, monuments, and other peculiarities of every district. Thus directed by the left hand, and spiritually led by the right, we drove through Södermanland, Östergötland, and Småland, through Skåne and Malmöhuslän, and we met with no accident until we reached the harbour itself at Trälleborg, from which it is obvious that on that journey we were escorted by a special favour of Fate. I could therefore say much of the ancient land of the Goths, but I am inclined to mix up a bit Nyköping, Norrköping, Linköping, and Jönköping, and I suffer from a sort of chaos about the Swedish kings; for there was a terrible number of them, chiefly Gustavs and Karls; and I would rather keep silence with regard to history, so as not to make any mistake. I only remember that the people of Östergötland have certain, or other typical characteristics, and those from Småland have others, but it may happen to be the other way round; but Östergötland is something of a broad, blessed, aristocratic plain, while Småland is a pleasantly undulating, poorer and peasant land; but both regions abound in a multitude of bushy and curly trees along the roads, and beside every human habitation, over the enchanted waters of the rivers and lakes, and everywhere, the earth forms a gentle hillock, or an intimate lap. All the time it is like the Lord's garden; but every other moment a granite boulder, overgrown with heather and juniper, breaks into this fecundity, erratic blocks lie scattered, a bare rock raises its head; all the time that monumental prehistoric stone world which blossoms everywhere upon the gentle and bucolic Swedish earth.

And then right at the end of the journey does the Canaan of the North open out before the pilgrim, the flat, and fertile region of Skåne, with its windmills and long avenues, a region spangled with piebald animals, and spacious farmyards, which contain stables as long as a factory, and barns as high as the minster at Lund; here the people no longer make buildings of wood, as in the rest of Sweden, but of stone, and of bricks tied with beams, and the fields bear heavy crops of wheat, large yields of beet, besides all sorts of the Lord's bounties whose place is on the table of mankind. In spite of that the inhabitants of Skåne remain faithful to a simple diet expressed by the ascetic formula "food at the right time, good food, and plenty of it"—nothing else. I have observed that wherever fine animals are kept, and ancient, noble

Södertälje

Bråviken

Linköping
Skeningen
(Skeppsättning)

Östergötland

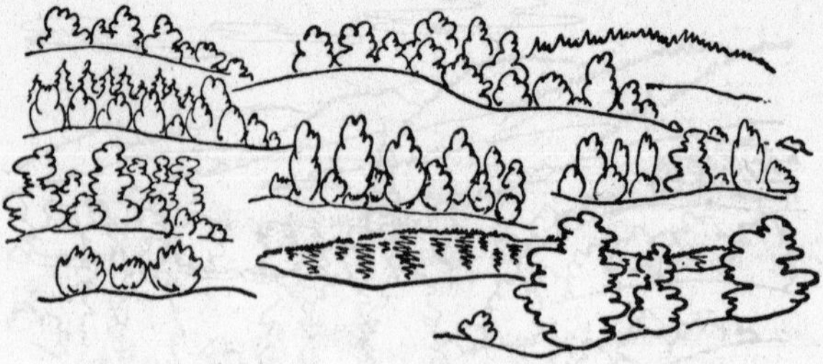

Småland

Vidöstern

Skåne

Skåne

trees are growing, there lives a superior race of men; and these Swedes from Götaland are truly great and noble farmers. So you see, the end of the journey; and the circle rounds off. From the sweet Danish land all saturated with milk like a pink udder, right up to the edge of the world, where nothing else grows but a handful of tiny Arctic plants among the stones; and over the Arctic tundra to the green pastures, and dark forests; we have combed this stretch of the journey with the open palm of the hand, as when a man goes by a cornfield, and lets the ripening ears slip between his fingers; in Norrland no doubt you would have to bend a good deal to stroke the oats. And here in Skåne the circle closes; again already the gods of herds and of fruit bless the traveller—as they did on the other side of the Öresund.

NIGHT

It is night again, and over the Baltic broad flashes of lightning betoken fine weather. Past the green and red lights, past the blinking buoys and the glare of the lighthouses, the illuminated hotel afloat is bearing us to the shores of that other, that bigger Europe. And can you think what I should like to know? Perhaps it is only this, in which sund now is the *Håkon Adalstein* traipsing with flour, cement, and a handful of people; don't you know up there it is not yet dark night, the sun only sets in the flaming sunrise of the aurora. My word, it was a good boat; no floating palace, it's true, like this one, but instead, we people were much nearer to one another and to things.

I don't know what those nations are up to all the time with that power and greatness of theirs; well, well, don't you burst with all that pride! Here I have been to look at three nations—they are called small; and you see that their system is good, and if one were

to count perfect things one would find them there in greater number than among the larger terrestrial kingdoms. And here also history has produced any amount of hostilities, conquests and wars; and nothing of them remains; they were all to no good. Some day people will come to realize that no victory is worth while; and if they really are in need of heroes, they might take one like the small doctor from round about Hammerfest, who in the Polar darkness runs his boat around the islands where a woman is in childbirth and an infant cries. All the time there is scope for brave and complete men, even when one day the war drums cease to roll.

Well, night again, and above the inky sea flicker the

broad sabres of lightning; does it mean a storm, or fine weather? How immediately does the world appear more terrible and tragic when we look upon it at night! You see, man, these are no longer Swedish dusks, transparent and grey, and cool like the water in bays, nor the metaphysical vertigo of the midnight sun; this is already the very ordinary, oppressive, European night. Well, what about it, we went to have a look at God's peace, and now we travel home again.

A grey and cold dawn is beginning to break; it is something like as if one were to open a damp morning paper, and read in it what had happened again with the world. For such a time we have read no news; and nothing has happened, only a couple of weeks of eternity have passed away, the Norwegian mountains reflected in the waters of the fjords, the Swedish forests closed in above our heads, and the gentle herds gazed at us with peaceful, saintly eyes. The first ugly, and inhuman news, not until then will come the real end of the journey. (Yes, here it is: it just had to be that horrid misfortune of Spain! God, why does one love so much all the nations that one has seen!)

Through the grey dawn shine the lights of Europe. What can one do—this is now the end of the journey. Fishing smacks sail out from Rügen just the same as in Lofoten, except that their sails are a bit different. Now perhaps the *Håkon Adalstein* is sailing north between the bare rocks of Lofoten. My word, it was a good boat, and a good journey.*

* To tell the truth, it now only was, for in the meantime I have received this letter from the *kaptein*: "Nun ist meine alte dampfer *Håkon Adalstein* degradiert. Alle die Cabinen sind weghgenommen, auch den salong wo wir essen, nun sind sie nur führ ladungen. Es war traurig führ mich zu sehen, when ich meine alte dampfer liebte. Ich bin nun auf dem dampfer X.Y., laufen zwischen Bergen and Kirkenes mit post and passaschiere, aber diese ist nicht so gut wir meine alte." And be her memory honoured to the last full stop.

GEORGE ALLEN & UNWIN LTD
LONDON: 40 MUSEUM STREET, W.C.1
LEIPZIG: (F. VOLCKMAR) HOSPITALSTR. 10
CAPE TOWN: 73 ST. GEORGE'S STREET
TORONTO: 91 WELLINGTON STREET, WEST
BOMBAY: 15 GRAHAM ROAD, BALLARD ESTATE
WELLINGTON, N.Z.: 8 KINGS CRESCENT, LOWER HUTT
SYDNEY, N.S.W.: AUSTRALIA HOUSE, WYNYARD SQUARE